LET
THE
LIGHT
GUIDE
YOU

LET THE LIGHT GUIDE YOU

Dennis Johnson
From Death to Life

Dennis Johnson

XULON PRESS

Xulon Press
2301 Lucien Way #415
Maitland, FL 32751
407.339.4217
www.xulonpress.com

Xulon
PRESS

Unless otherwise indicated, Scripture quotations taken from The Message (MSG). Copyright © 1993, 1994, 1995, 1996, 2000, 2001, 2002. Used by permission of NavPress Publishing Group. Used by permission. All rights reserved.

Printed in the United States of America.

Paperback ISBN-13: 978-1-6628-1776-2
eBook ISBN-13: 978-1-6628-1777-9

Preface

———◆———

THERE IS A PROCLAMATION OVER A LITTLE southern town that everything is better there. What is considered "better" would depend on the Local's definition. And what is 'everything'? This little town is in the Bible belt where most folks live by the Golden Rule which, as one abides by it, can contribute to everyone's betterment. Not every town can boast about everything being better and it is doubtful this town or any town would broadcast information to the contrary. Remember Otis, the town drunk, in Mayberry? The sheriff and his deputy made sure drunken Otis was cared for by locking him in a jail cell. Citizens with a desire to keep their town's good name would keep Otis' disposition a secret, look the other way. Except for a few rolling of the eyeballs at the mention of his name, folks may nod an acknowledgment and continue their merry way.

Like the sheltering of Otis of Mayberry, there were citizens of this little town who sheltered the foolish, unwise decisions I made when I ran amuck through the town and across the countryside. Amazingly, only one public announcement was recorded in the local newspaper of a poor choices I made. Needless to say, my reputation followed me and there are people today who shake their heads and roll their eyes at the mention of my name; Dennis Johnson, a.k.a. Squirrel.

At a Bible study in this little southern town where everything is better, or so they say, I met a lady named Carol. I shared some of my story with her. After hearing about where I have been and how I got to where I am today, she suggested I write a book. I'm assuming it was the puzzled look on my face that prompted her to offer help in getting my story from my head to these pages. What no one realized would happen when we got started on my story, was the healing that would take place in some of the characters as their roles in my life unfolded. Most people try to bury their painful past; however, it has been said that 90% of healing is talking.

My desire is for you to see how, through no fault of my own, I innocently got into a vast hole, what happened during the years I spent in that hole, and how God brought me out of it. In retrospect, I maintain that God has been with me all my life, although unbeknownst to me at the time. I believe God knew that after climbing out of this hole, I would tell my story and I pray it is the key to helping you or someone you know to climb out of a similar hole.

> "One day you will tell your story about how you overcame that battle you went through. And God will send you the exact people who need to hear that story." (*Grace & Mercy Ministries, FaceBook post on 2/15/2020*)

Chapter One

M Y MOTHER, ELIZABETH WRIGHT, WAS BORN in 1938 when the minimum wage was 40 cents an hour for a 44-hour work week. It was also the year a non-profit organization was established by President Franklin Roosevelt to combat the polio epidemic: The March of Dimes.

The earliest history any of my siblings or I remember of our mother is she lived, for a time, in an orphanage. Her mother, Mary, contracted the highly contagious disease, tuberculosis, also known as TB. In the 1940s there was no quick cure and much of the treatment was fresh air, good food, and bed rest. Sanatoriums were built to house TB patients while they recovered. In 1904, there were 115 sanatoriums with the capacity for 8,000 patients expanding to 839 Sanatoriums with the capacity for 136,000 patients in 1953 (cdc.gov). Maybe my grandmother lived in a sanatorium for a while. Apparently, there were no friends or family upon whom she could depend to take care of her child, thus the orphanage was the best option for my mom, or so grandmother thought.

The story passed down through the years is that, unfortunately, mom was experiencing some form of abuse within the orphanage. It is tragic when caregivers take any devious and destructive advantage of naïve, defenseless children.

It is said that people who are desperate do desperate things and mom was desperate to leave the orphanage. Enter suave and debonair, my father Dad. Okay, he could have been suave and debonair unless mom charmed him to aid her cause. Their meeting and relationship could have been many things, positive or negative.

For sure, dad was a military police officer at the Hunter Army Airfield where the orphanage was located. From 1946-1949, many of the buildings at Hunter were leased as industrial plants, apartment houses, as well as the orphanage (Wikipedia). Maybe the Military Police were assigned the orphanage as one of their service projects. It could be that the servicemen supported it with picnics and game activities for the residents throughout the year. Nevertheless, no one will ever know how dad and mom met. Whatever she believed about my dad, he was her ticket out of her desperation and, at 14 years of age, she left the orphanage to marry him. My sister, Nancy, was born when mom was only 15-years-old. Which raises the question: How did she get permission to marry at 14? She could have been pregnant. At that time, being pregnant bypassed one's parents' written permission for a marriage license (Marriages: Trends and Characteristics, United States, p. 11). Maybe mom made my grandmother aware of the abuse and her only recourse was to give her permission if she thought she was powerless to provide any other alternative.

Often what many couples have experienced can be described of mom and dad's relationship. The focus of desperate circumstances as well as how to survive or escape them could have occupied mom's mind. Thinking wisely at such a young age through the mode of escape from the orphanage and beyond is usually not a timely issue. It is only after the escape that mom found there were more problems with which to contend than she could have imagined. The situation would regress as the participants were not prepared to walk into the future together.

What Mom didn't know was that, in his early formative years, her husband had been exposed to abuse as well as to non-age-appropriate activities. My grandfather had taken him to houses of ill repute when he was just nine years old. He would one day say the ladies there "entertained" him. That's when he started drinking alcohol. By the time dad was 13 years old, he was an alcoholic and had been sexually molested. He was also tormented by the demons that attached themselves to him in those circumstances resulting from the lack of protection from his father. As this story continues, one can see how the iniquities of the fathers are passed on through the descendants. Exodus 20:5 and Deuteronomy 5:9 talk about the iniquity of the fathers being passed down through the generations. Dr. Henry Wright, in his book *A More Excellent Way*, tells us that if we do not deal with what has happened in our family tree, and if we do not deal with what is in our personal lives, our children will inherit our curses. Therefore, my dad's heartbreaking history would eventually be ignorantly repeated in his own home.

Before he served in the Korean Conflict, Mom was known to say dad was the nicest person one could want to know as he was a caring, kind man. My parents had three children; Nancy, Richard, and me. The violence dad witnessed in Korea may have contributed to his alcohol proclivity and molded him into someone unrecognizable as a husband or father. After many stories from veterans and their friends or families, the atrocities of those conflicts were internalized by thousands of veterans. Their pain was so deep that many of them turned to drugs, alcohol and cutting themselves, as well as many other activities to escape their pain however temporary. More permanently, suicide was the departure of choice.

However, the stage was set for my dad in his early impressionable years by the abuse of which he was victim as well as the witness to how his dad lived life. His dad exposed him to the culture permeating the nightclubs, bars, and houses of ill-repute. His dad also put him in the ring to learn to fight grown men.

After dad's service in the armed forces, he would drink excessively to escape his painful past; the darkness tormented him and who he had become. When he was drinking, he usually got into fights. When the law was called, he would hide from them in the brush.

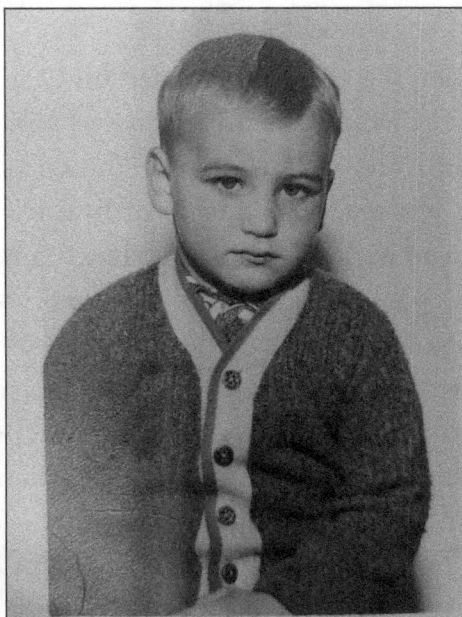

As a toddler, I drug my favorite blanket everywhere I went. It was security for me. I was holding that blanket, struck with fear and confusion, while looking out the window to see the police fight with my daddy. Dad continued to fight when they handcuffed him. I wanted to go out and help him fight the police. The little boy in me didn't know what my dad had done that was so wrong, and I wondered why the police would treat him that way.

There were incidents when Dad would drink and cut himself with a knife or glass. He would take the blood that oozed from those wounds and wipe it on my little face. I couldn't understand why my dad would do that to me. Could it have been the repeat offense of rejection that Dad had experienced at the hand of his father in his earlier years and he was passing on this belittling behavior?

As I grew older, the curse was passed on to me and when I would drink, I would cut myself just as I had witnessed my dad doing to himself. When he did cut, it was like a release…like whatever was inside of him that needed to come out, flowed with the blood. In Mark 5:5 is the account of the demon-possessed man. No one could restrain him; he couldn't be chained and couldn't be tied down. He had been tied down many times with chains and ropes, but he broke the chains and snapped the ropes. No one was strong enough to tame him. Night and day, he roamed through the graves and hills screaming out and *slashing himself with sharp stones* (The Message)." The demons would make the man cut himself as the kingdom of darkness operates on bloodshed. In the occult, blood is power. The more the demons could make him cut himself, the more power those spirits received (Ark of Grace Ministries)."

Because of dad's unpredictable behavior, mom would do what she had to do to survive and protect her children. There were many occasions when mom would take us and run to the safety of her friends, co-workers, or family's houses, in the car, or under a stranger's house while trying to avoid dad. He was mean and would beat mom. When she got away from him with the children, he would seek them out, so mom could sign over her paycheck. She was afraid that he could kill her, and he probably could have, but all he wanted was her money—he couldn't see anything else about her. With his intimidation, he made her his financial enabler and she felt she had no choice but to comply when he caught up with her.

My sister, Nancy, with tears streaming down her face, remembered the horror that took place one night. She witnessed our drunken father knock holes into the drywall with his bare fists then turn on our mother. When mom finally broke free from him, she instructed Nancy, who was shaking with fear, to sit between my brother and me as a means of protection while mom ran next door to use the phone to call the law. Nancy was about 12 years old and certainly no match to our dad if she had to protect us from him.

We witnessed our mom lock our drunken dad out of the house. In his aggression, he busted the glass out of the door with his bare hand. The glass deeply cut into dad's skin and caused a broad splatter of blood onto everyone and everything in proximity.

Chapter Two

SEVERAL YEARS AFTER LEAVING THE orphanage, mom found herself planning another escape—not with dad, but away from him. She managed to load us into the rusty red '54 Ford. She had not yet learned how to drive the manual transmission, but she had watched dad shift the gears many times. She knew that to get the car going there was a time to push on the gas pedal as well as a time to push on the pedal on the other side of the brake. The gears would grind while mom tried to shift them until the old car rolled on down the road.

Mom had loaded the rusted-out floorboard and the back seat with cardboard boxes filled with our belongings. Nancy, Richard, and I watched the blur of the highway through the floorboard. The car was loud because the muffler had broken off the engine some time ago. The exhaust fumes necessitated riding with the windows cranked down. Then the floor of the car got so hot the boxes started smoking. Thankfully a gas station appeared. The car didn't catch fire, but the boxes were scorched. The whole scenario could have been disastrous for them all.

We moved in with our grandmother. By this time, she had been well from tuberculosis for several years. Of the good things to happen in her life, the blessed best part was accepting Jesus Christ as Savior. She became firm about standing on the Word of God because it says in Isaiah 55 that His Word will accomplish what He sent it to do! I can remember grandma holding me in her lap while reading to me from her big red Bible and praying for me.

When mom got to the point she could manage on her own, she moved our family from Grandmother's house into public housing in Savannah, Georgia. A man named Lewis frequently visited her. During this time, I didn't know if my parents were even still married or not, so thoughts of dad coming home to find this man and becoming very upset flooded my mind.

When mom felt that our time in public housing was up, once again I observed her pack the car with our belongings. This time being even more careful than the first. We climbed into the old red '54 Ford mom had now learned to drive, and we went to Metter, Georgia. As we pulled up to a vacant house, I noticed another car pulling into the same driveway. The man I had seen come to our home in the Savannah projects and several boys I didn't know got out of the car. They brought their boxes and toys into the house as me and my siblings were bringing in ours. It was at this moment we learned that our mother had married her visitor from Savannah, Mr. Lewis Aldrich. I was eight years old at this time and didn't quite understand how we were to be expected to become one big happy family. My young and naïve personality would cause me to soon become a target for my new "brothers." They would often tease me about coming from the projects of the Savannah streets.

Thankfully mom's new husband didn't beat on her but they frequently fussed and argued. He was a good-looking man and known to be quite a cat with a tendency to be unfaithful to my mom. While he was friendly to everyone, he was not trying to be their friend. There was usually an ulterior motive which had to do with how he could capitalize on his relationship with them. I would experience this dark side of my stepfather. The trials of our home could be attributed to open doors to demonic activity through the abuse of alcohol, anger, fighting, and the iniquities of the fathers passed down through the generations.

This scenario has played many times over the course of history: A woman will have such baggage from her past that she doesn't think clearly about herself or her children. She focuses on finding a man to take care of her. Then when a man shows her attention, she unwittingly sees stars in his eyes, and stars all around everything he is or does; hangs on to every word he says with unswerving faith. He is probably charming and a liar. She has not taken the time to get to know him and marries after a short engagement if there's any engagement at all. When a wedding is planned, she thinks of all the cute ways her children can participate, but, wait, they have not been a part of the relationship. They have not been included to become acquainted with the gentleman or his family, particularly his children, if he has any. If there's a daughter, step-dad can overstep his boundaries with her. If there are sons, stepdad can treat them badly. It takes a special type of man, a godly man, to take on another woman's children and to raise them as his own in the nurture and admonition of the Lord.

Divorced, single mothers find themselves overtaken with car payments, insurance, rent, food and clothing bills. While finding themselves buried under mountains of bills, they are often forced to work more than one job. This leaves little time for her to care for her children and sadly enough, they are left in the care of those who do not always have their best interests at heart. These caregivers sometimes take advantage of the children. My mother found herself caught in this sickening trap with no clue that I would become a victim of her new husband.

Chapter Three

THE TWO FAMILIES BEGAN THEIR LIFE together on a small farm out in the country on Highway 121 north of town. There were cows, bull calves, chickens, as well as other farm animals. Since I was the youngest and always tagging along, I pretty much did whatever my older brother, Ricky, and stepbrother, Snooky told me to do. One day they put me on a bull calf in the pen. When they opened the gate, the bull calf took off wide open down the fence row scraping the fence trying to get me off his back. The bull calf put his head down and bucked one good hard time. I went flying! I used my arms to brace the fall, landed on my elbow and shattered it.

Children can get into all kinds of predicaments when their parents are away. Mom was working in Savannah and our stepdad was never home either. There were no cell phones in those days. Phones were few and far between with most rural folks having to go down the road to use the neighbor's phone. Even then, the neighbor might be sharing a party line and must wait his turn to make a call.

Having a shattered elbow caused me to have to lay around for hours. My brothers, left to nurse me had no clue what to do with me. They had seen me hurt before. I was a tough guy and didn't let anything get the best of me. Snooky warily looked at me and said, "Dennis, this ain't like you." Not knowing what else to do, the older boys kept picking at me and pulling on my arm saying it wasn't broken. None of them had been hurt like this before and nobody knew what to do except to tease me. As bad as my arm hurt, I tried as best as I could to fight them off. Finally, Snooky found a neighbor with a phone and called mom.

By the time Mom drove from Savannah, my arm was swollen. She immediately took me to the hospital where I was given a cast. When the cast was removed, my arm was still not straightened out. When the doctor said that it would be like that for the rest of my life, I found myself trying to encourage my discouraged mama, "Do not worry, it will be okay!"

Chapter Four

O NE OF THE BONUSES OF A STEP-FAMILY WAS having cousins My siblings and I had none that we knew of until the summer when David came to visit. David and his family had been coming to Georgia for vacation as long as he could remember. His dad and my stepfather were brothers. They were reared by a father who had iron fists, so to speak. He was a very hard man being reared hard. It was a dysfunctional family, to say the least, with very little love or compassion.

A native of Georgia, David's dad took employment in Texas and made their home there. Over the years, he would use his vacation time to take his growing family to Metter, Georgia, for two or three weeks each the summer. There were eight people in David's family. They camped for two and a half days along the way to Georgia in a Ford pickup truck long bed with a slide-in camper for the 1,000-mile trip. Pick-up trucks in those days did not have extended cabs, or four doors. There was only the bench seat in the cab where three people, maybe four, could sit comfortably so most of the family had to ride in the camper on the back of the pickup awaiting a turn to sit "up front." Needless, to say, when they got to Georgia, they escaped their mode of transportation like ants pouring out of a hill.

Making long distance calls in those days were problematic by today's standards but no one knew any different back then. Telephones were few and far between. The public telephone booth was mostly at a local establishment where everyone knew to go to make a call. Usually, one stood in line and waited his turn while listening to the one-sided conversation of the person talking on the phone.

If a number was unknown, the operator would look it up. The caller could tell her (for a very long-time woman were the telephone operators) he needed to make a long-distance call. He could give the name of the person he was calling. The operator would make the call and ask for the person. If the person wasn't available there would be no charge for the call. Calls were paid for with quarters, dimes, and nickels. There were two ways to pay: One was to put in the money as the operator directed. The second way was to call "collect". That means the person receiving the call pays for it. It's amazing how the operator knew just how much money was being put into the dedicated slots on the phone.

There were party lines as well as people just didn't have phones in their homes, yet. A party line was a phone line shared by the people on that line. Many times, when one went to make a call and picked up the receiver, there would be no dial tone but a conversation instead. If you were making the call, you would have to "hang up" and wait awhile to pick up and listen again. Everyone on that party line expected the other users to listen and hang up. Surely there were many nosey neighbors who pretended to hang up. Those who had phones were expected to let their neighbors use them as well as to relay messages for them.

So, for all the above information, therefore, about half the time, my mom didn't know David's family was coming for vacation—they just showed up. When she saw them pull into the yard and pile out, her facial expression reveal the gracious words trying to come out of her mouth.

"Visiting at Uncle Lewis' was always an adventure", David recalled. "Now that there were more children with which to play and one, Dennis, that was my age, the visits were anticipated with fervor by the Georgia-Texas relatives." Farm animals provided plenty of entertainment particularly when the boys attempted to ride any of the equine, bovine, or swine varieties. One of my jobs was to feed and water the animals as well as see to their care with David tagging along trying to help, but there were just too many distractions to stay focused on chores. We mostly played with the animals pulling their tails, or ears, chasing them, and teasing them to get response even if just to make them mad or scared.

The farm was near the Fifteen Mile Creek that runs under the bridge on Georgia Highway 121. Most of the area involving the creek was swampy and flood-prone. With all the trees, logs, stumps, mud and water as well as the wildlife adapted to those conditions, there was always much to explore and discover that only boys would appreciate. Snakes, lizards, squirrels, 'possums, and 'coons lurked about in the swamp. Once, I even found myself on the back of a five-foot gator, riding him about four feet before he knew he had a passenger. There was a nice swimming hole in that creek where we spent a lot of time on those hot summer visits, gator or no gator.

David and I were a united pair and not afraid to take on trouble. When we were about 12-13 years old, we would hang out at the pool hall in town along with other kids. One day this kid began teasing David and it escalated to the point when I said to David, "He's going to have to take us both!" The three of us rolled out the door into the parking lot with fists flying. We fearlessly won the row, giving credence to my budding reputation as a fighter.

Cousin Dennis recalls:

> "After Dennis and I became young adults, he came out West to work for a little while, drinking all the way. It was winter time and a blanket of snow covered everything. When he got off work that evening, and since he had no experience working in the snow and he was drinking on top of that, he left his work boots on the porch. They should have been cleaned off and brought inside. When he went to put on his boots the next morning, they were nowhere to be found. Tough, but unwise, and hung-over, Dennis went to work barefooted. When he climbed up on the roof to make an installation, the boss walked by.

He noticed Dennis' bare feet and asked about why he was outside without his boots. The boss man was either desperate for help or was kind and compassionate because he told Dennis to get into his truck that he was going to get Dennis some brogans.

Rough and tough Dennis—after one of the times he got shot, my wife and I went down to Georgia to visit him. He wanted to go deep sea fishing. We loaded up, liquored up, and went to the coast with his staples still intact; but as we fished, the staples became lose when a wave washed over him and opened that wound."

"The fishing trip David speaks of was after I was shot with the .44 Magnum. We were about 50 miles out in the Atlantic Ocean. The seas were rough but, as usual, a couple of half gallons of liquor later board a big boat, no one was worried about anything. A big wave hit us, and it pushed me against the rail of the boat. Two or three of the staples I had all the way down the center of my chest popped loose and I began to bleed. I didn't let that stop me from fishing. I just poured some liquor on it. The boat's captain wasn't happy with me bleeding on his boat. We stayed out there another hour or so. When I got home, my mama was mad. I just put a bunch of those wide

Band-Aids over it and took another drink, and another, and another..."

David ends his interview with these heartfelt words:

"When I heard about the lady who was helping Dennis tell his story, I desperately wanted to let her know how I feel about him, how much I love and respect him. Despite his upbringing and unfortunate reputation of that season, he is a good man. It is obvious the change that faith in Jesus Christ has made in Dennis as well as the whole lot of those people mentioned in his story. I am proud of Dennis, proud of his personal accomplishments, and I am proud to call him my friend."

Chapter Five

MY STEPFATHER DID HIS BEST TO SEE TO IT that us boys stayed busy and out of trouble, despite our access to and the love of alcohol. He worked us like we were grown men. From farm chores to anything else he could find for us to do, we stayed busy. Vacation time came for the Texas kin when he was building his club on 121 north. He had us out in the hot sun digging the septic system by shovelfuls, no other tools. It was four feet deep and 10 feet wide. The farm chores and added work at the club kept us boys continuously working.

Gaining height, weight, and strength, required us to help with or do the harrowing, tilling, planting, harvesting and all necessary machine maintenance at each phase of the season or any breakdown in between. I can smell the oil I used many times to repair and replace moving parts, sharpen blades, replace or rig worn tools. A farm family's day always began before sunup and our family was no exception. We didn't watch TV because we didn't have one.

Being the mischievous boys we were, we managed to sneak in some horseplay when we thought we could get away with it. We loved the adventure too much to concern ourselves with the double trouble headed our way if were ever got caught.

During the cold weather, the only heat in the house was a fireplace. My brothers and I cut and split firewood all year long. It was kept on the porch and by the fireplace in the house. Thankfully, that wood warmed us twice—once while we were cutting and splitting and the second time when the wood was burning in the fireplace.

When I was young, I thought my stepdad was mean and cruel. In later years, I came to the realization that he was trying to teach me to work hard and to be responsible. Every young boy desires to have a relationship with his father. The need is there to be mentored. The void in my life came because my biological father was not present. My step-father carried wounds from his own past and thus, was unable to fill that void.

I was given a nickname because I could run fast and climb a tree like no other. "Squirrel" is what they called me. Ricky and Snooky would make me go up the trees with a cane pole to knock down the green pine cones. They would take the cones to the forestry and sell them. The forestry harvested and planted the seeds which were used to grow seedlings for replenishing the pine forests. Pine tree farming has been a prolific operation in the South. Pines are grown for utility poles, fence posts, and pulpwood for paper-making. Pine needles are used in landscaping. Selling the seeds was a good way for us to make some spending money.

On our summer vacation visits, David and I liked to go fishing anywhere we could cast our bait and the Altamaha River was our favorite spot. About an hour and a half south of the farm, it featured sand bars, alligators, otters and other river interests. We have walked that river within five feet of 'gators. After I got my drivers' license, I bought a VW bug. A trip down the dirt road to the Altamaha was always an adventure. When we reached the sandy road to the river, I would quickly turn the steering wheel to the right then to the left making the car swerve from one side of the road to the other. The amount of sand on the road could have made it really easy for the car to flip. When we got to the river, we got out of the car laughing and slapping each other's backs. Our dads were not happy with us. That was a tail beating I won't ever forget. Despite the spanking, hot-rodding was a favorite pastime for us! We even cut doughnuts on the courthouse lawn in the dead of the night. Even as I was growing into a young man, I was always just a big kid at heart!! I sought out adventure with little regard for who, what, when, and where. Except for the trip to the river and the work at the club, my stepdad spent very little quality time with me. David held tight to his uncle's attitude, actions and words concluding that he was a "powder keg waiting for a match to light it." We all walked on eggshells around him.

Chapter Six

T HE DAY I SHOT MY BROTHER, LANNY....A.K.A "Snooky."

"We were out in the woods. He had a loaded .22 and he handed it to me. The *Smith and Wesson Safety & Instruction Manual* explicitly reads, "Never pass a firearm to another person until the cylinder or action is open and you visually check that it is unloaded" and "Accidents are the result of violating the rules of safe gun handling and common sense." Well, we didn't read any of that so in whatever way he handed it to me and whatever I did to receive it caused it to fire. The bullet took off the tip of Snooky's nose. He hollered and carried on until someone came and took him to the hospital. While it was an accident, I got whipped for it. I was the scapegoat many times for the anger, resentment, and frustration that so often is placed upon stepchildren for whatever reasons. It didn't matter to us that we were stepbrothers. We were always together doing something. We got along just like real brothers and I loved him."

Snooky's unintentional retaliation:

"On the way to school, Snooky dropped me off at a four-way stop near the school. When he made the turn, he didn't look to see where I was, and he knocked me down with the car then drove over me. The tires went over my legs. He must have felt it because, he stopped. When he didn't see me, he backed up and ran over me again. Then he realized what happened, jumped out of the car, and got me out from under it. I couldn't walk. No bones were broken but I was in the hospital about a month with both of my legs severely swollen and the doctors monitored me for bleeds."

Little did I know Tracy would end up being my wife...

"Tracy's sister, Vickie, was dating my step-brother, Broadus. Vickie would come over to visit and Tracy would come with her; but Tracy would not get out of the car despite my efforts to encourage her to get out and play. Once she had a piece of bubble gum she shyly shared with me. I thought she was pretty and my interest in her was sparked. From that very day, there was always a little spark between us. Every day at school, I looked for sweet, quiet, reserved little Tracy. We both lived in town at the time. Then my mom and stepdad bought land on 121 North and built a house in the country. Before long, Tracy's parents bought land and built a house right down from us. We became neighbors and grew up together."

Tracy's dad tolerated me at first, because he remembered when he himself was a young teenager with much to learn and energy to burn. I was always rippin', roarin', and smokin' either in or on some type of motorized vehicle going by their house. Riding motorcycles was a favorite pastime on the farm. There was plenty of riding room and I made sure to find a few minutes to ride between chores. Not being old enough to legally drive yet never stopped me. In the country, children learned to drive at a young age to move farm equipment between fields. It wasn't long and I would become a nemesis to Mr. "Tracy's Dad," particularly when I began showing interest in Tracy.

Chapter Seven

NORTH OF TOWN ON GEORGIA HIGHWAY 121, few who pass would be the wiser of the history of the modest Hispanic church on the right. Our stepdad built a supper club there- which was a quarter-mile from their house. In those days, maybe the early '70s it was called a juke joint. In addition to our farming responsibilities, he had us cleaning the club on Friday, Saturday night, and Sunday morning after closing. We didn't go to church on Sundays because we didn't know anything about church at that time.

The supper club was a cement block building. We worked long days pouring the concrete floor and someone else laid the blocks. At the time, as it usually does to a child, the building seemed huge. The front had big tinted glass windows. The doors, which were also glass, were an accident waiting to happen. Surely people would get drunk and get thrown through them and that's exactly what happened. Eventually, Mr. Lewis replaced the glass doors with wooden ones. There was a long bar with a cooler box behind it that was about the length of the bar and it stayed filled with ice-cold beer.

Bands from near and far found the club an easy venue in which to display their budding talents. It's exceedingly doubtful any of them made it to the big times. They couldn't even finish a song without drunken fights breaking out; and I, being about 13 years old at the time sat at the bar observing all the dark activities.

Sadly, during the supper-club days, the drunken women knew that I was naïve and inexperience. They found excitement in taking advantage of me. They would charm me and take me out somewhere to have their way with me.

When our stepfather built our house, he saw to it that there was a bar inside there, too. When Christmas came there were always different flavored half-gallons of liquor at the house. That's where every holiday was celebrated—around the bar with family and friends. My favorite memory is the pride I felt when I would see my mom dressed to the "T" for the holidays.

My story continues:

"At this time in our life Mother worked at a car dealership in Savannah. She drove back and forth between Savannah and Metter for 15 years. She was a hard-working woman. Since she was gone 10-12 hours a day, we children mostly raised ourselves. When she got home from Savannah in the evenings, she still had to work in the small kitchen behind the bar at the club. She did all the cooking. Because we served plenty of fish suppers, we would get 200-300 pounds of small catfish and clean them.

Many things went on at the joint that Mother knew nothing about; one of which was my stepdad mostly paying me in alcohol for all the work I did. I was always drinking and drunk along with Ricky and Snooky. We were a threesome. We were mean, crazy, fearless in most instances, and we were always in mischief. When we lived in town, my brothers and I played hooky from school. We would hide in the attic all day long looking out the window for stepdad. He drove a bread truck, so we had to keep a lookout for him, we knew we had to hide and keep quiet when he would come home for lunch or come home early. When we moved out in the country, we grew our own pot, smoked cigarettes, and drank moonshine. THAT was a big deal. If you did that, then you were doing something!!

We *did* have an occasion to show *some* civic pride. We were not all bad all the time. We had a couple of neighbors, two alcoholic men who lived in a sure enough shack. They were two cards shy of a full deck and exposed to various types of ridicule from the community. They would come to our house and press their faces to the window looking for something to eat. One day when they came over, my brothers and I loaded them into the back of the pickup truck and took them to the creek. We backed the truck into the water, took the clothes off the guys, and gave them a bath scrubbing them good with soap. Neither of them liked it very much. We cut their shaggy hair, unruly eyebrows, long fingernails and toenails. We had gotten new clothes, new socks, and new shoes for which we had pooled our money and we proudly dressed those guys. They still didn't like it. About a month later, when he realized he had not seen the guys, Snooky found them dead in their shack. We blamed ourselves for the stress we put them through. The effect of alcohol is probably what killed them along with the stress of people's abuse."

Chapter Eight

⟨⁓•◆•⁓⟩

MY GETAWAY PLACE TO BE ALONE WAS THE field next to the pond across the road from the club. There was an old Ford Falcon that was ONLY field worthy so that's where we drove it: in the field and to go fishing. About this time cars were beginning to have sunroofs and I wanted one, too. With a cutting torch, I cut a sunroof into the Falcon. Okay, it was a sunroof-shaped hole! One night when I was parked in the field, I built a fire and was drinking. I stood up in my homemade sunroof and told Satan to come in and I would serve him the rest of my life. Then I saw the black-hooded figures dancing around the fire celebrating their newly confessing convert.

There were many nights that I was made to sleep at the club to keep watch over it. I was so scared to stay there by myself that I would drink to get the courage. My stepdad gave me a .38 which I tucked into the back waistband of my pants. He told me to shoot anyone who broke in. Even though I drank to get the courage to shoot if I had to, it wouldn't have done any good to try to shoot someone because I would drink until I passed out.

On the weekends, I had more friends than I could count because I had all the alcohol they could drink. They weren't even that interested in being my friends. They were more interested in the alcohol. They could drink all they wanted and brag about it. They would put up their tents in the field across from the club. They would camp, build fires, tell jokes and stories, just talk, drink and brag until the sun came up.

When I cleaned the club after a weekend of partying, I would take out the trash along with cases and cases of beer and fifths of liquor to hide in the cornfield, so me and my buddies could indulge in them. I could drink all I wanted just to keep the place clean. Inventory was no issue…no one was sober enough to pay attention to inventory of any kind of food or drink.

With the availability of alcohol and my desire to partake, I believe I was probably a full-blown alcoholic by the time I was 14 years old. Often suspended from school for fighting, I was not a studious student and academics were nowhere near my forte. With all the farm/club responsibilities, I rarely had any time for homework; however, my reputation for fighting was becoming more solid.

I was never too proud to work and always looked for opportunities to pick up some cash. As a young teen, I delivered bread, picked tomatoes, and worked in tobacco. I always had a little money on me and drove some nice older cars. My Mother taught me how to buy cars on time and to pay back the loans.

"A man named Wiley helped raise me since I was 13. He was about 15 years older than I and drove nice cars. He looked after me a lot and was like a big brother. When I wanted to earn some money, I would go up to his chicken farm and pick-up eggs. He and I had some memorable occasions one of which is when I had learned how to make moonshine. One evening, we had a load of it in the bed of Wiley's truck. The Feds showed up in a black car that had a little red light on top of it that was going around and around. This truck had a 454-big block. We scrambled into the cab as Wiley said, "Hold on, Squirrel!" and we took off, dirt flying behind us. A tire flew out of the bed and went rolling down the hill in the field. We spun through the sand behind the chicken houses; that's usually where we went to hide from the law because we knew they would not bring their cars through there. We stopped at the edge of the field. I jumped out of the truck and ran into the woods to hide. From my hiding place, I could see the sheriff and his boys running through the woods looking for me.

Eventually they caught me. Shamelessly, I kicked the sheriff in the shin. Then the deputies hand-cuffed me. They were all big dove hunters back in that day and we all would hunt together. We had that kind of relationship: I would be running from the sheriff and his deputies, one minute and we would all be dove hunting together the next. My mother had always told me I needed to leave town, because of my reputation: always fighting, always in trouble with the law. My older brother told me that he felt like I had inherited a gene or something and I was going to grow up to be like my dad. Mom was clueless that her boys needed a father's affirmation and guidance. She could only encourage us to be and do better.

"Family trees are very important diagnostic tools. Behavior… problems tend to repeat themselves. We see patterns repeated from mothers and fathers to their children…Exodus 20 teaches about the sins of the father being passed on to the third and fourth generation. Psychologists also have observed certain personality characteristics and behaviors such as rage, anger…that can roll over to the next generation (Wright, 68).

Chapter Nine

EVERY WEEKEND, MY RUNNING BUDDIES AND I would ride out in the country late at night. With no fear of us getting caught, we would steal a hog or two. If a big party was planned it would be 2 hogs but small ones. We would load them into whatever vehicle we were in and take them to the Fifteen Mile Creek which, at that time, ran with fresh, clean water. We gutted, skinned, and cleaned the hogs then we took the meat to the shooting range where we had a pit dug for cooking. We gathered with all our friends, cooking, eating, and drinking.

We raided chicken houses, cleaned and cooked the chickens, boiled the eggs, and ate all of it around the fire. There were no McDonald's, Burger King's, or anything else fast food and we had to eat to survive. Away from the bars and juke joints, this is what our fun was. Whatever meat we had, we cleaned it and cooked it while hanging out around a fire pit. This was FUN! Summer or Winter this was our good clean fun.

I sit and wonder at the mischief. Yes, even then the Lord had His hand over us all—my running buddies along with my brothers, Ricky and Snooky. Right in the middle of our hot mess, God was with us!

I rode my motorcycle a lot and rode it to school on the last day of 8th grade. I drove it up the steps, through the doors, and 'wheelied' into the school. My favorite teacher, Mrs. Youmans, didn't turn me in, though. She was very lenient and tried to guide me, so she overlooked many of my shenanigans.

My wife, Tracy said, "Dennis was so handsome; there were teachers who would flirt with him. His good looks more than likely, got him off the hook for his mischief."

Back then I could just fall off my motorcycle into a ditch from being drunk and many times I would be drunk when I drove into the yard. Mother knew that wherever I was trouble was inevitable because I was usually drunk. She would call the law as soon as she heard me drive into the yard. When the officers came, they would try to handcuff me, and I would fight them. I remember them putting me in the backseat of the squad car and I kicked out the back window. Sometimes I even jumped out of the car while it was moving with my hands cuffed in front of me. They would stop the car and chase me.

One night I remember the guys quickly hauling alcohol out of the supper club, then it caught fire. After the embers cooled, Snooky and I recovered the alcohol that was salvageable. We sold it out of the back of the car on Sundays unbeknownst to my stepfather. All the bottles were covered in black soot, which didn't bother the people who were buying it. They got it at a huge reduction in price; so, what's a little soot with great savings?

My stepfather built another club, but it didn't stay open long. Trouble was constant. People were coming from different counties and causing fights with the locals and with each other. Guns were always going off and ambulances were coming in and out. On those nights I hid behind the bar; I was so scared I was going to get shot. Nonetheless, Step-father had confidence in his young teen boys to keep the peace at the club. We were the club's bouncers. We were bouncers bouncing grown men. Sometimes we were successful at it and other times not so much.

My stepfather encouraged me to fight for money in a big square "ring" out in the field: real fist fights that drew blood. There was something about fighting the men and the all the bloodshed. It was almost like I liked it. It has been said that when a man lacks his father's affirmation, he becomes either passive (fearful of new challenges) or aggressive (focused on affirmation by achievement) (Eldridge, 2001).

I knew I had demons in me from drinking all the alcohol and I felt I gained strength from it which was evident when, one night at home in the bedroom I shared with my brothers, I woke up. At the foot of my bed stood a black figure with a hood…an 8-9-foot demon. I couldn't tell much about it except the glowing red in its eyes scared me. Strangely, at that moment, I picked up the chest of drawers full of clothing and threw it.

Most everyone referred to me as "Squirrel." People from other towns would come and bring their friends. They were coming to fight Squirrel because I had a reputation for fighting. I loved to fight, especially when I was drinking because alcohol gave me confidence and, seemingly, super-human strength. My buddies and I were at a keg party on the banks of the Ohoopee River at a small community near Oak Park. Most of the Metter gangs, at the time, were there. Gangs then are not what gangs are today. A gang was a group of friends who were near to one another with much of the same interests in which they participated together. There was no competition between the groups; however, while we weren't interested in fighting each other, a fight could break out just because there's an unfortunate misunderstanding about something and the effects of alcohol heightens the situation. And, this night, a couple of the guys got into a fight. One of them tried to leave in his car. The guy he had been fighting broke out the driver side window trying to continue the fight. He managed to drive off and left the scene. No one knew the guy was going for reinforcement. Apparently, his gang had not yet arrived. Soon I heard a vehicle approaching and turned around to look that way and saw a truckload of men drive up with shotguns. There was only one way in and one way out and they were blocking the road. They were looking for the guy who had busted out their friend's window. The guy who busted out the window was hiding down beside the bank next to the water. Another buddy of mine at 6'4" was a fighter, too. In defense of the guilty fellow and full of "courage", he stood up and said, "I'm the one you're looking for." The guys in the truck jumped on him and I jumped in, too, loving every second, at least until I got hit in the head with a piece of pipe. The blood was all in my eyes; I couldn't see anything. By then I was fighting blind. They beat me down and tore my tail up. I got away and climbed under my friend's Cadillac. Those guys stuck their knives in the tires with me under the car. When they left, my buddies jacked up the car and I crawled out. This is just another time when God had me; I could have been severely injured. Listen to me. This is God working in my life. He was with me and has kept me all my life. As I look back over the years, a lot has happened to me. I do not see how in the natural realm I got through any of it. I do know Jesus was with me every step of the way. He allowed Satan, the enemy, to do whatever but he could not take my life.

Both parents told me to get out of the house more than once while I was living at home. I was disrupting their life with my rebellion and penchant for trouble when I was drinking. I was always drinking because alcohol was easy to get.

At that time, I was in good physical condition, I could lift the front end of my stepdad's tractor. I made a punching bag with ears of corn and a croaker sack in the barn. I beat that bag so hard the corn came off the cob. I would hang my feet under the rafters of the barn to do pull ups to keep my stomach like a twelve-pack.

I worked out with weights every chance I got. When working in the fields, I often would throw 100-lb bags of fertilizer off the truck. Yep, back then I was built. I had a friend in Savannah who taught me Tai and Jui Jitsu. He tore my butt up many a day. One day he quit teaching me. When I asked him why he said, "Because you're getting too good!" I paid him in alcohol. We would hit one another hard enough to draw blood and we used our bare fists—never boxing gloves, tape, helmet, or mouthpiece.

Chapter Ten

FOR MOST OF MY LIFE I HAVE LOOKED FEAR IN the face and did not shy from it. The higher the adrenaline rush, the better. Even at a young age I always enjoyed fast cars and bikes. When I commandeered whatever vehicle, I had at the time, it was hold it to the floor or park it! I had a 1972 Chevrolet Nova. There was a two-step chatterbox on the steering wheel which is a lot quicker with the finger than the foot. Every time I pressed that thing the wheels would come up. While it was a lot of fun, I never wrecked a dragster. I knew when and where to respect the power of an automobile…most of the time.

Drag racing was always my high. No drinking was allowed during the racing season. I did have a little sense to keep safety first at least with racing. Off-the-strip drinking was okay in my mind. I have said it before and I will continue to say it: I've looked back on the many times God has had my back and it makes tears come to my eyes every time.

My brother, Richard, remembers:

> "Mother worked at the VW dealership in Savannah, Bill Usery. She would get her Ford serviced at the VW place and Bill would lend

her a car to drive home. One of those times Bill gave her a brand new yellow 1972 Beetle to drive back to Metter. Mother was cooking dinner and needed some milk. She was too pre-occupied with cooking to think about how many vehicles Dennis had wrecked when she told Dennis to go to town to get the milk. She threatened him with sending Lewis and the boys after him if he didn't get back soon. Dennis picked up his buddies. They were all drinking moonshine and went out toward Aline. Then they decided to count how many mailboxes they could run over. When Dennis had not come home in a reasonable amount of time, Mother called the law. They didn't find him and his drunken buddies until Sunday afternoon, 24 hours later. The law called mother and told her: "Miss Elizabeth, we have found Squirrel and his buddies. Miraculously, they aren't hurt even though your car is totaled. They mowed down over 20 mailboxes which is a federal offense. We won't prosecute if you go back to these places and replace the mailboxes. I'm only doing this for you, Miss Elizabeth." She called her boss, "Bill, I totaled your vehicle and I'm sorry". He said, "No problem, Miss Elizabeth, it was covered under insurance. I'll send somebody to get you." There was a rare occasion when life threw her roses: that same year Mom received the Southeastern Parts Manager of the Year Award for Volkswagen."

Remembering my first marriage:

"The last year I was a teenager, I married a girl from Claxton, GA. We were together about a year. We had no children. As a surprise to me, she had me served with divorce papers while I was on my job. Then, I got with a woman, Betty, who was an alcoholic. She was 15 years older than I and a nice-looking woman. We stayed together about a year. When we split up, I flew out to Texas with my friend, Mike, to build hog farms for Mr. Jack. That was one of the best times of my unregenerate life. No one knew me. I always had a woman with me, sometimes two. When I came back home for a visit, I foolishly rekindled the relationship with Betty.

Mike and I flew out to Oklahoma to work for Mr. Jack. We stayed at a motel for a while. Betty wanted to come but I didn't want that. Later she sold all she had, even her typewriter that she loved, to get a plane ticket. Although she was a smart woman in many ways, she also loved to drink, even worse than I did. I picked her up from the airport and she stayed about four months. I didn't want her there with me because she was cramping my style, so I schemed a way to get her to leave. I asked her if she would sleep with Mike. The scheme worked because she got mad and told me to get her a plane ticket. I took her to the airport and as she was boarding the plane, she looked at me like she could kill me and said, "You WILL regret this!"

Mike and I stayed in Oklahoma a few more months. Surprisingly I saved more money than I spent and bought a Cadillac before leaving. With a pocketful of money and except for a few rest stops, I drove all the way home. All that steady driving blew up the battery; it was over-charged. We were overcharged, too, drinking all the way.

As soon as the word got out that I was home, Betty called and said she wanted to get back with me. I told her I was through with it. Little did I know how much SHE wasn't through with it...

...I was 21 years old on the night of the Georgia-Florida football game. Mother and my step-father went to see Hershel Walker play. As soon as they left, I picked up my buddies and we went to town drinking and getting high on Quaaludes. We were sitting in my car talking with some other friends in the middle of downtown where the old glass phone booth once stood. Betty's brother pulled up and called me over to his car, "Squirrel! Come over I need to talk to you!" I had forgotten her threat and had no clue that the man was there to avenge her. I was about a foot away from his car window when I saw the barrel of his .44 Magnum.

He had it cocked and said he was going to kill me. I asked him, "What for?" and he said, "My sister." It flashed through my mind I had to buy me some time. I quickly looked down and told him something was wrong with his hubcap. When his eye moved in that direction, it gave me a fraction of a second to turn. When he fired, the bullet entered my side and blew out my back. I staggered backward and went down. I was mad and on fire. If I had not turned, the bullet would have hit me in the chest. I got up holding my guts in my hand going after him with my other hand to grab his throat, but I went back down which was a good thing because he was going to shoot me again. Then, he sped off, burning rubber.

My friends picked me up and put me in the back seat of my Cadillac. I believe the drunkest one, Joey a.k.a. Wormy, drove me to the hospital. It felt like I had a glowing red-hot piece of iron stuck in my body and there was nothing I could to about it. I was sweating like it was raining. I knew I was dying. Before we got to Metter hospital, Wormy hit the brakes and I fell in the floorboard. I felt the hot blood sloshing on my arm…that's when I lost consciousness. My friends told me later when the ER personnel came to get me out of the car and put me on the stretcher, the attendant felt on my neck for the carotid artery pulse, then put a sheet over my head. They pushed me into the hospital and said I was dead. However, probably because of my youth, they gave me blood and shocked me. In the time I was dead, I went to Heaven. I didn't want to come back. I remember a bright light came through and put my feet in another world. The colors were vivid! It looked like Christmas lights on steroids. It was so beautiful! Don't doubt Heaven. I'm here to tell you, it's real—-I've been there!

My brother Richard reminisces:

"Joey called Mama and told her about Dennis getting shot. Mom and I went to the Metter hospital together to check on him. When I first saw him, he was laying on a gurney with his arms hanging to the side. I could see his intestines gushing out his back. He was dead. The more blood they pumped in, the more it kept flowing out of him! I didn't know what shot they gave him, but once they gave it to him, he sat up and started talking. At that moment there was no more bleeding."

This reminds me of a story about my grandfather. Once when I was a toddler, I was with my daddy and his daddy at the pool hall. They were involved in a card game. One of the other players thought my daddy was cheating. Daddy stood up to confront the man and that is when the man shot him in the gut six times. At that moment, my granddaddy immediately took daddy out to the car, spoke into him and the bleeding stopped. This seemed to be a supernatural gift.

Airflight flew me to Memorial Hospital in Savannah where I immediately went into surgery. That is when I had a heart attack and died.

The saga continues:

"I heard the Lord talk to me and I felt boldness. I had no stress, felt no shame. All I could feel was love. There were the most vividly beautiful colors. Although people were all around me, I couldn't see them, but I could feel their presence. It's hard to put into words. Then I heard Jesus tell me I had to go back. I told Him I didn't want to. Then, I woke up…four months later…with a sheet over my face. I pulled the sheet off and there stood a priest. At that time, I didn't understand who he was, what he was doing or why he was doing it, just that I was in the hospital. I remember the little round hat thing on his head. He was holding a Bible and sprinkling on me what I later learned is called holy water. The cold water on the sheet soaked through to my skin and it woke me up. I pulled the sheet off my head and when I looked at him, he ran out of the room. It was very quiet there. I had on no clothes, just a sheet. I started reaching to see what I felt wadded up under my back. It was cotton and packing gauze. A flood of doctors came in. My mom came in crying. I didn't understand what they were doing but apparently, I died and came back to life.

I was moved from that quiet, peaceful room into an intensive care unit. They started hooking me up to the noisy machines that beep 24-hours a day. To my vanity's horror, a colostomy bag was attached to my abdomen. I must have looked like Frankenstein with what seemed like miles of tubes and plastic bags hooked up to me. My skin was discolored. A tube was down my throat and what was coming through it was nasty and I'll leave it at that. I was in that hospital for over a year with my own little Christmas tree at Christmastime. Back in those days patients could smoke cigarettes in their room so I did. That was when healthcare institutions allowed tobacco use inside their buildings.

I didn't know the Lord then, but He was the One who brought me back to life. Everyone said I was lucky, but luck had nothing to do with it. God has a call on my life and was preserving me to get me to that call.

My mom gave me a .25 automatic pistol because I got a phone call from the guy who shot me telling me he was going to finish me off. I said, 'Come on because I'm going to kill you and your whole family!' Except when I was drinking, I never wanted to hurt anybody in my life, much less kill 'em. I had it in my mind when I was able to get out of the hospital that I *would* kill him, and I planned for a long time how I would do it. When I looked in the mirror at myself with a colostomy bag and my face all sunken in, I looked like a skeleton. Then, I got really mad!

Upon discharge from the hospital, I went to live with my mother. I was given several bottles of

Betadine solution with an irrigating syringe with which I had to flush out myself in the bathtub at home. I wanted to go out, get a girl, but I could not begin to see myself on a date with that bag attached to me no matter how badly I wanted to.

When the fall of the year came, it was cane-grinding time and that's exactly what it's called except it is said, "cane-grindin'." That's when the sugar cane is ready to come out of the patch (a very small area in the field). When I was a child, a mule would travel around and around the grinder while the cane was being fed through it. However, today modern conveniences have replaced the mule with a tractor.

As it was being pressed through the grinder, the can juice would flow into a bucket. The full bucket would be emptied into a huge iron bowl that was about five feet across and sat in a hole over a fire. The juice would be boiled and skimmed to remove trash and impurities. When the juice reduces to syrup, it is ladled into bottles and capped off. A 'cane-grindin' is usually a time when friends and families come together for fellowship. Depending on who is the host and who is invited, it can turn into a party. This time it was a party, so I joined my friends cooking syrup, eating biscuits, drinking liquor and getting drunk.

Eventually the colostomy bag came off and I started eating my mother's good country cooking. In time my weight returned and I started working out again. I still had staples but didn't let them stop me. I was disturbed about my appearance because I was particular about looking fit and good which was cash-in-hand with the girls.

A few months later my stepfather said, "Squirrel, I have a 270-deer rifle with a scope. Go get that son of a gun (not his *exact* words) who did this to you." I took my deer stand and set it up near where he lived and started watching for him every evening. My thought was to shoot through the windshield right into his head. I did this for three months, day in and day out. Then after a while I didn't see him anywhere. Finally, someone told me he had gotten word I was after him, so he left town and I never saw him again.

After that I started carrying a pistol on my side—wouldn't go anywhere without it. I told myself I would not be shot again unless I could shoot back. I wasn't the type who wanted to kill but after that experience I said I would be ready if there *was* a next time. I was not saved, did not know or have a personal relationship with Jesus. Proverbs 20:24 says, "A person's steps are directed by the Lord. How then can anyone understand their own way?" Even then God was with me and

I had no clue. He is the reason I am still alive today. I give Him all the glory because I look back now at the row I hoed and how I lived my life. I should have been dead and gone to Hell so many times. But my Savior had and still has a plan for me. For my Heavenly Father, my Abba Father says in Jeremiah 29:11: "I know the plans that I have for you. Plans not to harm you but to give you a hope and a future." Praise God!

The pistol I carried with me was for my protection. The law never bothered me about it. I'm not boasting about myself, but the law seemed to be leery of me. I guess because they knew I would fist fight, not with guns or knives. When they would turn their blue lights on me, I would stop and ask them what they wanted. They always knew I was drinking and wanted to make sure I got home safely.

My stepfather bought a Philips 66 gas station downtown and I started working there. That's where my Cadillac was parked, and I wouldn't drive it because of the bloodstains in the back and it bothered me. My step-brother was in Satan's Savage's motorcycle gang at the time and wanted to buy it, so I sold it to him for $80. As I worked at the station I got my muscles built up again by changing heavy truck tires. I was practicing fighting again. My weight got back up to 175. My colostomy was gone and when I took off my shirt, the scar shone like a badge of honor.

I have been shot on two separate occasions by two different men. The world would tell me that I should have hunted down these men and gotten revenge. I am thankful to God for the way he kept me through both situations. I trusted Him to take care of these men for me. In God's Word, He tells us that vengeance belongs to Him. Hold your peace and let Him fight for you!

Romans 12:19, "Dearly beloved, avenge not yourselves, but rather give plae unto wrath: for it is written, Vengeance is mine; I will repay said the Lord."

Chapter Eleven

In our early teen years, Tracy and I went our separate ways probably much to the relief of her father. She left home when her parents were divorcing. So, her ticket out was to marry someone who showed her attention, had a car, and some money. She married one of my friends but, I never felt he was good enough for her as he didn't treat her right. He was an alcoholic and would beat on her. From time to time, I would see this man at the pool hall. Our meetings always ended in a fight! During the time he and Tracy were married they had a daughter, Shalane.

Tracy was still married to her first husband when I was shot with the .44, she and all who loved me were afraid I would die. She kept up with me through my mother while I was in the hospital. She didn't want to be too nosey. She wanted to call more often but she was still married and was hesitant. Tracy said, "I can remember the last time I talked to your mother. It wasn't looking good for you and I was afraid you could die at any moment."

After a few weeks, Tracy heard I was out of the hospital. When she found out I was home, she would call me; but when I answered, she would be too nervous to talk and hang up. Eventually we would meet in town in the park and just talk. Tracy had always loved me and said I had a good heart. She saw the good in me; something that many others could not see.

The relationship between Tracy and I began to blossom. Tracy separated from her husband and moved in with her dad until her inevitable divorce was final. My first fight after getting out of the hospital was with Tracy's ex-husband and brother-in-law in front of the pool hall. The ex-husband was mad that he had lost his family. I put a good whippin' on them both. I loved Shalane like my own. Her father didn't support her. I would eventually have a conversation with Shalane's father assuring him that I would take care of her and that we both needed to grow up for her sake. From that time on, there was no further agitation between us. When Shalane was old enough to go out with her friends and got into troublesome situations, she would call me for help. The two of us connected and became close just as if we were biological father and daughter. While I was always ready to rescue her, the one rescue I couldn't make was the night Shalane died in a wreck in 1999. Until I became and remained sober, I spent many drunken nights crying at her grave, "Even though I knew she was not there."

Tracy and I spent more and more time together until I asked her to marry me. We eloped to the Rock Hill, SC, courthouse in 1982. "Her daddy didn't want me to marry her. He knew how I was and, looking back, I don't blame him!"

Dear friends, let us love one another, for love comes from God. Everyone who loves has been born of God and knows God.

1 JOHN 4:7

More escapades:

"I had just bought a black 1980 Chevrolet Z28 Camaro. The paper tag from the Auto Mart was still on it. I was drinking of course and driving too fast around a curve. I lost control and landed in a pond. I thought I was going to drown and then I started thinking, "I messed up my good-looking car!" A man in a pickup truck came driving by and stopped to help me. He took me home. Then the "Georgia Boys", the Georgia State Patrol, arrived with a sobriety test. It registered at .13%. The GSP was going to handcuff me for DUI and called the local sheriff for backup. I don't know who was talking to who, but the sheriff's department told the GSP to leave me alone. That's been a long time ago and that's just the way it went down. The lawyer saved my license, but it cost me $1500. Regretfully, I sold my car to the junk yard. She was a beauty, low to the ground and would run 145 mph. In the short time I had her she performed well for me!

Not too long after the Camaro fiasco, I had been hog hunting and stopped at Jay's Truck Stop to get gas. I was about to be on my way to go help drain a pond for the fish when there stood three dudes, acquaintances. I heard them talking very low and when I passed by them, I felt the tension. I came right out and asked them, "Y'all wanna fight? Let's go around the corner and I'll fight you." One of them replied, "No, we don't want to fight you." Another one went to a red Ford pickup with a gun rack. He pulled out a single barrel shotgun. When I saw it I thought, "Uh-oh, here we go." I turned and started back to my car then I heard the sound of a gunshot and felt the sting of the pellets as they dug into the skin on my back. I got to my vehicle, pulled out my pump shotgun and pulled out the plug. I had slugs not buckshot and I knew if I hit one of those guys it would tear them to pieces and I was not a killer. When they saw the gun, they started running and hit the ground. One was hiding under a truck. He was crying and pleading, "Don't kill me!" I shot the ground next to him then "water" ran out from under the truck—he was so scared he wet his pants.

I would later learn that the people in the restaurant were hiding under the tables and other places fearful of the shooting going on outside. Three of my slugs were found near the gas pump and one near the boy's truck.

I threw my gun in the back of my car, got my buck knife out and was trying to get the BBs out of my arm. I couldn't get to my back. I had to do something to deal with the pain, so I poured liquor all over me. I went to my sister-in-law's house. She was a nurse, but she would have nothing to do with me. Her husband drove me to the hospital, dropped me off and left. He didn't want anything to do with me either. He didn't want anyone to know he was related to me. He later told me he was scared he would lose his job if anyone knew he had taken me to the hospital that night because it was going to be in the newspaper. The policemen came to the hospital and took me to the police station. They were going to put me in jail. I particularly wanted to be back there with the guy who shot me. He wasn't back there and they weren't going to lock me up with him anyway. That's when they grabbed me to put handcuffs on me and I wouldn't let them. I flipped them and kicked them, injuring them in their groins.

When they were all laid out on the floor, Gene Sherman told me to leave because I just disrupted his jail and hurt his policemen. I started walking away and my stepdad pulled up beside me. He called me a few names and told me to get my behind (not exactly the word) in the truck. He took me back to the jail. With no assistance from anybody, I put myself in the cell with another fellow. The next morning, Sheriff Bell came up there. After he heard the story, he asked his deputies, "The four o' y'all couldn't lock that man up?"

In the cell I was sitting on the trashcan and noise was coming from it. Sheriff Bell asked what was going on with the can. I got off the trashcan, popped the top off, and my cellmate fell out. He had crossed me during the night, so I picked him up, put him in the trashcan and put the lid on it. The sheriff said to his jailers, "Y'all know to lock Squirrel up by himself. He can't be locked up with anybody else 'cause he's too uncooperative and cocky."

I was wearing no shirt and blood was oozing down my back. Sheriff Bell took me to the hospital. He said I could have killed somebody. He also said I needed to go to rehab but rehab wasn't open that day. Sheriff Bell was like a father to me. He would sit me down from time-to-time and tell me what I needed to hear. I will always respect him for his considerations on my behalf as he was never about controlling me but about helping me get to the place where I could control myself.

Sheriff Bell said in his interview:

"I was much acquainted with them—Dennis' and Tracy's domestic situation. Every time Dennis got drunk and acted like a fool, Tracy would get scared and call me and that was at least once a week. I would go out to the house, cuss Dennis out, preach to him, and tell him like it was."

Finally, a life-changing event happened on Mother's Day, 1992. *The Metter Advertiser* reported it as follows:

Robert Biggers shouted, and his mother, Memory Biggers, and other family members looked up to see a 1979 Ford Mustang fly through the air, bounce once, hit a 1974 Dodge pickup parked in the yard with three passengers in it, spinning it around. The Mustang came to a halt in the top of a dogwood tree which it had hit and uprooted.

Memory Biggers and several family members were in the front yard of her home just outside Metter about 4:10 p.m. Sunday, where their Mother's Day gathering was breaking up. Some had left, some were leaving, and some were standing around in the yard when Raymond Dennis Johnson, 34, of Rt. 2, Metter, lost control of his vehicle, according to the State Patrol report.

He ran off the roadway traveling 137 feet before getting back on the road, crossing it, and traveling 205 feet before striking the pickup in the yard and spinning it around. The Biggerses, who witnessed the accident, said that it sailed through the air, at least four feet from the ground.

The State Patrol report said that Deborah Calhoun, age 36, Georgia Christian Calhoun, 12, and Wesley Calhoun, 44, all had visible injuries. According to Memory Biggers, they were sitting in the parked pickup awaiting the arrival of another…family member.

Sheriff Homer Bell reported that Johnson refused treatment at Candler County Hospital. He was placed under arrest and taken to Candler County Jail where he was charged with DUI, driving too fast for conditions, and driving with a suspended license. He is out on bond, Bell having released him to a family member Sunday night.

People were hurt because of my rebelliousness; someone could have been seriously injured or worse, killed. Sheriff Bell came to me and said I needed to go to rehab or I was going to prison. I said I would go and he took me to John's Place in Statesboro. While I was there, we, the residents, attended a small Baptist church. One Sunday the pastor preached on David and Goliath. I was intrigued with the story about the boy with only a slingshot against a nine-foot-tall giant and I was interested in the story because they were fighting—I was all about that.

I finally found myself in the courtroom before the judge when we had to go to court about this matter. Judge Ogden Duremis, raised his voice and sternly told me, "Dennis, THIS IS NOT THE O.K. CORRAL! It is NOT okay for you to be a fighter and a gunslinger!"

The judge sentenced me to pay three weeks salary for the policemen I had beat up because they couldn't work. He sentenced me to 470 community service hours since I had never been in court. That was the most community service hours to which anybody in Candler County had ever been sentenced. My service hours were spent with Leon Hadden, helping him mop floors at the hospital. He knocked off a lot of those hours. I remember him telling me, "Squirrel, I don't want you up here mopping floors. Just stay out of town for a little while." Maybe Leon didn't want to be around me either, maybe he was afraid someone would walk in and I would "erupt" at some point putting his life, health, and/or reputation in jeopardy…won't ever know because he passed away. The last few years before Leon passed, we often had the same conversation about those days: how I lived my life then in comparison to how I live for Jesus today.

Chapter Twelve

"From somewhere, surely it was the prayers of the saints, I gained an interest in approaching the door of the Metter Church of God when services were being held. I would just touch it, turn around and run off. I said to myself I have never feared anything so why was I fearing this. I did this three times and on the third time, I went inside. The building was full of people and Pastor Warren was preaching. When he saw me, he stopped and everybody else turned to look. Then he went back to his message. When the message was finished, people went to the altar. Grown men were there crying. In my opinion, grown men didn't cry. When the service was over, I was the first out the door. What I wasn't aware of was Tracy had those people praying for me—they went to the altar crying in thanksgiving that God was answering their prayers for me.

But something kept drawing me back to that church. I didn't know anything about the Holy Spirit except when I died after I got shot with the .44 magnum. I called it The Rim. I've heard people call it The Tunnel before you get into heaven. I felt no pain, no shame—it was like the best high I have ever experienced. When I got shot, I did not know Jesus.

The third time I went back to the church was a charm. When the preacher had the altar call many people there were crying. I didn't know what was going on, I just knew I had to step out and get there. When I stepped out, I said, "Lord, have mercy on me" and I have no recollection of how I got to the altar. Surely, the Holy Spirit took me there when He saw I was ready to go. All I had to do, all anyone must do, is to take the first step. The people in that church knew me and knew I needed the saving, transforming power of Jesus Christ. They all lovingly surrounded me and lay what felt like thousands of hands on me as they prayed.

Just as John could not stand before the glory of Christ's appearance (Epp, 1969), I met Jesus and found myself on the floor. Jesus cleansed me. All the baggage, the years of turmoil and corruption were gone. I was free! Hallelujah! I could see—my spiritual eyes were opened. Every day I thank God He saved me from the pit of Hell!

And suddenly I understood why those grown men had been crying at the altar. I cried then, too, and I've been crying ever since. I was a changed man. It also brought back to my remembrance of when I was a small boy. My grandmother had a big, red Bible with a cross on it. I knew even then as a small boy there was some sort of Power in that Book.

It seemed like every year I was in and out of the hospital from getting shot or cut up from fights, totaling out cars—that lifestyle was leading me straight to hell, but my Heavenly Father has a plan for me. I did not know it all those years ago. Jeremiah 29:11-14 says 'For I know the plans and thoughts I have for you, says the Lord. Plans for peace and well-being and not for disaster. To give you a future and a hope. Then you will call on me and you will come and pray to me and I will hear your voice and I will listen to you. Then with a deep longing you will seek me and require me as a vital necessity and you will find me when you search for me with all your heart. I will be found by you, saith the Lord, and I will restore your fortunes and I will free you, gather you from all the nations and from all the places where I have driven you, saith the Lord.'

I am not proud of how I treated my boys in their early years. Neither am I proud of how I treated my wife. I did not have a relationship with my Heavenly Father then. I didn't know how to be a daddy to my boys that could show them love. I didn't know how to love because my daddy didn't know how to show me. The saying is, "Hurting people hurt people." My boys say they have seen a change for the better since about 2008. They both say a whole lot of restoration has begun in my immediate family. If I could take it all back now I would. Although Shalane and I were close, I still didn't know how to be a good step-daddy to her. I guess I did the best I knew how to.

I look back on my life today and I can see on my journey that God was involved all along before I ever knew it. I saw all the many times I should have died. Through my own understanding I don't know how I came out alive from all the car wrecks, fights, and gun shots. God has restored me giving me back 10 years of my life. I don't know how people live without Him. We have new grace every day. He is faithful when we are not. He died for me and for you. His body was beaten and bruised for us for our healing. His blood was shed for me and you, a new covenant. His blood was shed for my sins and yours. What kind of love is this?

In the interview with Pastor Warren and his wife, Bonnie, at their kitchen table, Sister Bonnie mentioned that my step-brother had commented several times to her and the Preacher about how his dad had treated me in those early years. They had no idea at the time what kind of a monster was being created within me. The reason the Warrens came to Metter to preach was to reach the meanest in Metter. "That would be me!"

Words from my wife:

"I saw first-hand the state of mind Dennis was in when he drank hard liquor. He was a totally different person—a stranger to everyone. I called the sheriff's office many times and Sheriff Bell would come out when I couldn't take any more from Dennis, was just too scared of what he could do to me, or I would call the preacher, Brother Warren, to come pray—and Dennis didn't care for the preacher-types of visitors.

I felt I had to walk on eggshells when he was asleep because if I woke him all those spirits would awaken. Dennis would rant and rave, fume, cuss, and fight at the drop of a hat. When the preacher came over, Dennis would be so mad his eyes would turn blood red and he would just talk, making absolutely no sense. He was probably talking to those alcohol-related spirits who were agitated because the preacher walked in.

In those stressful, dysfunctional trying times when Dennis was living in the world with alcohol and drugs, cutting himself and/or fighting that drew blood, there would be an odor on him like the smell of sulfur or something rotten. I believe in evil spirits and the Bible calls them unclean; they can carry an odor. God gave me discernment of spirits: seeing, hearing, and smelling. I could feel my spirit rise in boldness when I could smell this. I didn't know at that time what it was or how to deal with it. But I did remember to call out to Jesus for help, protection and for Dennis to be set free.

Tracy wanted to keep her family together and she wanted me to come out of the snare of the devil that had held me captive and make Jesus the Lord of my life. She felt strongly that she needed to get into the church and pray. In that day, when somebody needed to get into the church, all that was required was to retrieve the key from under the doormat at the pastor's house. She got the key and entered the church. She had our two boys at the altar of the church praying for God to intervene in our marriage. If I drank there was *never* peace of any kind or in any measure. "Beyond a shadow of a doubt," says Tracy, "as my sons have gotten older, they have held it against me that I didn't leave their dad because they were exposed to his abuse and stupidity."

After a time of pouring out her heart to God, Tracy and the boys left the church building. As she returned the key to its place under the doormat, Sister Bonnie came out of the house and asked Tracy if she had heard anything that afternoon about me. When Tracy indicated that she had not heard anything, Sister Bonnie proceeded to tell her that she just received a phone call and was just walking out the door to the church to get Tracy...

"That was the last time I got shot. It was with a .22. The bullet went right beside my heart. This was in 1996 or '97. My cousin shot me. He wasn't in his right mind at that time, he really wasn't himself. We were at his house, both drinking. He was mixing something into his alcohol. The neighbors were fighting with him. They came to his house to continue their fight which I got into and beat them all. When I left his house, I forgot my cooler. He was standing on his back porch and told me he would shoot me if I came up on the porch. All I wanted was my cooler and to leave. Even though I didn't go near him, he shot me anyway.

Somebody called the law. The deputy sheriff, Gene Sherman, drove an unmarked Ford Mustang. He loaded up my shot self and hauled it to Metter hospital while yelling, "Don't you die on me, Squirrel, we been through too much, you hear me, Boy? Don't you dare die on me! You hear me, Boy? You hear me, Boy? Stay with me, Squirrel! Don't you dare die on me!" The actual words he spoke would not be appropriate—know what I'm saying'?

Eventually I would learn that I was airlifted to Memorial Hospital in Savannah and that I had a heart attack during surgery. That was the time of the out-of-body experience where Jesus took me to the rim of Heaven. The colors were beautiful. There was a feeling of love in me, on me, and around me. However, I was heart-broken and distraught when I awoke because I had been at the spiritual rim where I could see lights, trees, grass. Then, I saw my wife's brother. As soon as I could speak, I told Tracy I needed to talk to her sister Vicky about their brother in heaven. I told Vicky what I saw. She went to their mother, Annette, who said, "Yes, I had a baby boy that died at birth." Tracy had never heard that her mother had lost a child. She asked me how I knew it was her brother. I told her I saw it in his eyes.

I was kept sedated for a few weeks and stayed in the hospital for a few months. When I finally woke up it took a little while before I could remember what happened. The doctors came around to talk to me. I thought they were going to discharge me. They told me my heart wasn't stable but that was of no concern to me. I could see it in my mind I would be unhooking IVs, tubes, and leaving the hospital against medical advice to get my hands on my cousin who shot me. And that's what I did—I left. The pain I had in my body was unbearable. When I made it outside the hospital I sat down and smoked a cigarette. My family came out to try to get me to go back inside. All I could think about was going to get revenge. I went back in alright—I signed myself out. I thought I got along just fine but the repercussions would raise their ugly heads in later life.

I always kept a .357 between the seat and console of my pickup. Then one day Tracy and I were driving through town and I spotted my cousin walking on the side walk. I turned the truck around quick. I remember Tracy saying, "Oh, no!" and I said, "Oh, yeaahh!" I drove around the block and came up behind him. When we finally made eye contact, I said, "Today's your day, ain't it?" He froze in his steps. I really didn't want to shoot him. I just wanted to put my hands on him. I could hear Tracy praying and I knew my steps were still being ordered. He walked away and I drove away. I am thankful nothing went down that day. I surely didn't want to go to prison. I had a family. God intervened. A while had passed and the news came to me that my cousin had died. Isaiah 41:12-13 in the Amplified Version reads, "You shall search for those who quarreled with you, but will not find them. They who war against you will be as nothing, as nothing at all. For I the Lord your God keep hold of your right hand; (I am the Lord), Who ways to you, 'Do not fear, I will help you!'

The people who shot me are dead now. Even the girl that had me shot with the .44 died from an overdose. I never could figure out why anyone would want to shoot me. Tracy always said it was not like me to carry a gun. I really didn't care to carry. It was my stepdad who encouraged me. He always said, "Squirrel, them people ain't got no sense. They're out to kill ya!"

Tracy continues:

"After Sister Bonnie came to the door and spoke to me, my only thought was, would Dennis survive *this* time?

In the ER at Metter hospital, he kept trying to get off the table saying he was leaving. It didn't bother him that he was shot, he was still trying to fight. He wasn't going to let anyone help him because of the influence of the alcohol. People were saying he had been shot but he wasn't going down.

After I got to the hospital, I was not prepared to see that Dennis' neck was as big as his shoulders. I never saw anything like it. I was scared and crying. The nurse told me to calm down and get myself together that even though Dennis was sedated he could hear everything.

Brother Warren was sent to Metter for many reasons. One of those reasons was Dennis Johnson. Dennis was a part of God's plan for Brother Warren's mission effort because Dennis was on his way to Hell.

Brother Warren shared his thoughts with me,

"I remember looking at your step daddy, your mother and two stepbrothers and how dysfunctional y'all were. Your stepdad was trying to make a man out of you, but with the dysfunction, Satan was trying to destroy you all. I remember going to Dennis and Tracy's house. I walked up to the door and knocked. Tracy met me at the door and said, "Brother Warren, Dennis is at it again." Many men from the church came to pray that day. Dennis was hiding down in the ditch behind the house. I remember telling Tracy, "I don't know how you stay with that man." Tracy trusted in Something bigger and better and knew there was good in him.

I personally knew what Dennis was fighting because I was raised the same way. I knew in my heart, if God could reach me, He could reach anybody. God told me if I could get the most wicked, meanest people, the church would fill up. When I started the old church, I was threatened by one of those wicked men who wanted to do nothing but beat me up. Our pasts were similar although mine wasn't on a barstool like Dennis' and I wasn't provoked to fight, but I knew what God could do and He would do it for him. Dennis' stepdad was a hard man. He was raised like the way he raised Dennis. Deep down Dennis' mother was stubborn. Between her and Dennis' stepdad, they were always at odds. Dennis, as a youngun, was being shown a path and he decided this was the way of life and he better learn how to live it; he responded from his history of abuse.

From what I have been told, Dennis' real dad seemed to be a good, hard-working family man until he went into the service. When he came home from Korea, he was a monster.

A few believing-in-Christ-Jesus friends decided to meet for Bible study out in Dennis' shop where he kept his racecar. He would push it outside so we could meet. Dennis and Tracy needed someone to hold on to. I didn't want to see them lost. I had seen them come too far. Some will leave and go back to the world and I was not about to surrender them. God knew Dennis needed to hold on.

A storefront building came available and there the mission was born. From the storefront, the church purchased land and built a beautiful church named Metter Community Fellowship. Today that church is renamed Restoration Worship Center. We had no clue what great plans would take place for His glory, building the Kingdom and sending people from the east, west, north, and south.

Satan had Dennis' footsteps to start off with. Now God says, "I've ordered your footsteps, dark things are being revealed." God shows us things for a purpose. All his life Dennis had locked doors in his mind. He began to question. God shows us things to strive for. There is a reason for ALL things. Jesus gave us back our mind. We are torn back and forth. God will give us a little bit all in time. And when you get older, you'll see the roles people played in your life. I think the lifestyle Dennis' lived is way too deep for people to grasp; the kind of man he is. God speaks to Dennis and shows him things, things he doesn't understand but it's all in His timing. God will allow him to understand when he needs to understand. God's plan for Dennis will come to pass. The most important thing is our relationship with God. God is training Dennis beyond his fleshly capabilities.

Paul in the book of Timothy he wrote the last time. They had already prepared to come get him. You can only imagine what Paul was shone when he was on the ground. He was a mere man. When he got where he was going, God changed his mind. They made fun of him, beat him. Dennis is a modern-day Saul. His name has been changed from your street name to the name you have now. Paul was just as head-strong for running after God. We as Christians are called upon. There are people you can reach that no one else will be able to."

Chapter Thirteen

"IN 2000, TRACY AND I LIVED IN AND MANAGED an apartment complex in Richmond Hill, GA, for two years. We worked there together. I mostly painted, cleaned, and remodeled the units. Tracy was mostly the secretary. She worked hard to keep the apartments rented. We enjoyed our work and learned how to do business as well as how to manage people. Our testimony was that God moved us there to encourage the people we encountered.

We weren't ready to leave our Metter support group; we weren't grounded in the Word yet, so we became stagnant in our Christian growth. We weren't in fellowship with the body of Christ. We didn't even try to visit a house of worship. We weren't taking the Word in, so we couldn't give it out. We stayed to ourselves outside of work. We were doing everything right as far as running the facility. Then, the complex owners came falsely accusing Tracy of not doing her job. She had never made any move without consulting the owners and they knew it. Even though she was hurt, she took it as God moving us on to another chapter of our life.

I got a maintenance job with Pierce Parts and Service out of Macon. Since I was paid very well, we did some enjoyable things. We lived right down from the river, so we had boats and a pontoon. During this time, I began having chest pains. I thought it was indigestion, but I knew something was not right. That same year I had a five-by-pass surgery. I was 42 years old and was told I had a heart of a 90-year-old man. After I recovered from the surgery, I had to find a job that was not so demanding.

With my family and a drag car in tow, we went to work in an alcohol and drug rehab center in Soperton, GA. I was the director and Tracy did her secretary thing. We went there to help men who had strongholds with drugs and alcohol even though I still had strongholds in those areas. I was not using at the time. There were about 35 men in residence with access to woodworking and mechanical shops on the campus. They kept the grounds nicely manicured and attended the Bible study time we offered to them. I thoroughly enjoyed working with those guys.

While the center supplied us with a home, our food came from donations from other churches and food banks. Our physical needs were met. Part of our spiritual sustenance came from pastors representing churches in the area. They would share the Word and pray with us all in the small campus church.

This is where I met my good friend and brother, Ricky Brantley. He was serving on the board of directors at the Christian Family Center. At first sight we really didn't hit it off. Ricky would talk with every man who came there and ask a few pointed questions one of which is "What brought you here?" All he knew about any of the men was what he heard them say. If one listens long enough, one will learn about people who will tell many things about themselves. Ricky told me I didn't have to tell him anything and that he would just listen for three days; then he could tell me all about myself.

Ricky recounts:

"In our conversations, Dennis would talk about all his former possessions and what had happened to him including how he had been shot multiple times. He told me he had gotten to the point where he would never have to work again. Five or six years later some things came against him that he didn't foresee coming with medical situations and no health insurance. He got too busy drinking then his job started sliding away and he was financially ruined. He told me about his heart attack as well as other troubles. From what I could put together, they had lost everything. I watched him and didn't like him from the start.

He and Tracy worked with the man who owned New Life Center. He let Dennis and Tracy live in a fixer-upper mobile home in exchange for the work on it. After talking to Dennis for a while, I concluded that he also needed to be in the program there. I would have thrown him out based on what I saw Dennis do and heard what he said. But, the Lord let me have enough discernment to see what I needed to see. I felt Dennis' heart wasn't in the right place and he didn't really want to be there. Eventually, we would spend time together talking and in fellowship which would lead to friendship.

Dennis acquired an Old Chevy II drag car—a full race car. He would work on it instead of working with the guys at the center. The guys at the center tolerated him. Some of the guys in the program came to me and said Dennis was drinking. He swore to me he wasn't, and Tracy asked me about he twentieth time not to give up on him. During that time, it was rocky with Dennis. He said to me more than one time that it was a good thing we didn't meet earlier in life because one of us would be dead. The Center was thinking about telling him to leave. He seemed to be taking advantage of riding that free horse and his wife was doing everything she could do to hold it together.

One Sunday morning Tracy called and said Dennis was going to the drag races. It made me mad right off the bat as I focused on the fact that it seemed everything that we had talked about was in vain. Dennis was going to the race instead of taking the men to church. I was hurt that he would do that and mad beyond explanation. If I could have gotten to him, I would have burned that car and wore his tail out. Then I realized those actions would not help him, that Dennis needed a change from the inside out.

Tracy was quiet and sweet. She asked me to give him time; so, I put up with Dennis. I put up with his junk. There are a few people at the most that God has put in my life that I really wanted to throw away and God said "no"; Dennis was one of those. You cannot help someone who doesn't want to be helped.

I backed away from him and went about my business. After awhile he finally realized it. Conviction came on him because of what the car was doing to him, to the center, and to his relationship with the Lord—it was a hindrance. The devil will use things we like to side-track us from the things that we would love, such as a real relationship with God. I know because I travelled that road myself. That's probably why every time I would do the mental throw-Dennis-away thing God would say, "Don't."

My wife and Tracy became friends and another chapter was added to our story together. We began to hang out and get to know each other which gave me more time to talk to Dennis, to try to figure him out. We would go out to eat supper and fellowship. Tracy's desire was to hang out, so Dennis could see how it was supposed to be—how normal couples interacted with each other to build friendships. As time went by Dennis and I got to know each other well. Both of us were interested in the racing world and I came to love him like a brother. He was ready for a nicer place to stay and I was ready to help him."

Reminiscing about the center:

I walked the same roads those boys were walking. My heart felt all their hurt which brought up my own hurts that I thought were buried deep down within me. I tried to fight the fight but was not grounded where I should have been although on several incidences I knew the play of the game. There was a convenient store just over the hill from the center. Late at night a few of the boys would ease out and go purchase beer. They had no idea I was watching and waiting for them to return. When they did, I poured out every can they had. They didn't like who I was either. I felt as though I had failed but I got back up again and again. It's not important how many times you fail, what is important is to continue to get back up. Even though I was not where I needed to be, I know in my heart God used me in my mess.

Chapter Fourteen

TRACY AND I PURCHASED A HOME WITH LAND in Dublin close to Ricky. For several years, I worked as maintenance man for sixteen Subway restaurants in the area. Tracy worked at one of the stores as a store manager. Then we moved back to Metter where the "rubber meets the road." I was tired of my lifestyle of indecisions and sitting on both sides of the fence:

With my early walk with the Lord, I was falling and getting up time after time. I knew I had to make the decision to say, "Enough is enough!" I was sick and tired of the yo-yo life. The night I was struggling with these thoughts, I threw myself on the floor in the living room and asked God to heal me or kill me; I could not continue my lifestyle, I could not do this on my own.

Immediately, I thought God was killing me because I could not get my breath; but He was breathing life back into me. Scared to death, I jumped up, ran out of the house, leaped over the steps, got in my car and just left. After a minute of driving, I thought, "Why am I running? I feel free, I AM free!" God spoke to me and said I was delivered from Legion. I had never heard of Legion. I shared this with Tracy and she told me that name is in the Bible and it means *many*.

I rode around in my car for a long time. All the windows were down, and I knew I had very large angels riding with me. I called them, "my boys." I'll never forget this time I experienced with my Jesus, my Savior. Thank You, Lord!

God established a new covenant with me pouring out His Spirit upon me, so I became united in purpose with Him and empowered to maintain righteousness. I had truly become a child of the Most High. God took away the heart of stone and gave me a heart of flesh that is responsive to God's touch. Ezekiel 11:18-19 says ...*and I will give them one heart, a new heart and put a new spirit within them. I will take from them the heart of stone and give them a heart of flesh that is responsive to My touch. That they may walk in my statutes and keep my ordinances and do them. And they shall be my people, and I will be their God."*

Losing the ego:

> "I really thought I was a good daddy to my boys when they were young. My idea of a good daddy was to keep a roof over their head, food in the house, pay the bills and buy them a car when they were of age. The important thing I didn't do was to be a real daddy; show them love, affirm and hold them. I was an addict and an alcoholic during their formative years. I was not taught how

to love or how to show it; therefore, I didn't know how to give it. It has been said that one cannot give what one doesn't have. I have seen the love of my Heavenly Father. I am a student of His love. Now I am aware of showing my love and my Heavenly Father's love to my boys even though they are men now. I've asked their forgiveness and they tell me, "Daddy, we have forgiven you." If only I had known how to love them and spend time with them when they were small maybe they would not have some of the issues they have faced. Tracy always had the boys in church. They cut their teeth, so to speak, on the pews of Metter Church of God.

I've been clean and sober now for twelve years. I was a prideful and rebellious man. Before Tracy and I married, I loved to drink, loved women, fast cars and loved to fistfight. Fist fightin' was the man-to-man way to fight. This day and time there is so much cowardice. Young men must have their knives or guns. My mother, God rest her soul, was a hard-working woman and prideful as well. She took care of bills while my stepdad played with bars, gas stations, and farms. I know I said this but it's worth repeating: my step-father was hard, but he taught me how to work, to stand on my own.

A man takes care of his family. I've worked all my life, most times making good money, until my health started failing from all the abuse I have brought on myself. I've lived in the moment drinking, drugging, and chasing after a good time with women. Having cool-looking fast cars, just whatever I wanted to do and wherever I wanted to go, that was my lifestyle. If trouble came it was because I was holding up a reputation. I took care of things the only way I knew and that was to fight, fist-fight. It's not like that today. Look at someone the wrong way and get called a racist or get shot and maybe get killed. The older I get, wisdom and knowledge come.

When money got tight, I did what I've always known to do—get out and make money. I know *how*, it's just get up and do it. I knew when I set my mind on it that it was the wrong thing to do but I was going to do it regardless—I would just get back in business like I had years ago, but I knew I didn't have all the tools I needed to get back out there with people, the realtors, just getting out there with the public. I went to pawn shops for tools and then I got a job replacing some flooring.

I had just had a total knee replacement about four months earlier. One of my sons and I were going to do this job together. He told me he could do all the work. I wouldn't have to get on my knees and I could lead him through the job. It sounded like a plan and that's what we were doing until it came to a point when I thought I had to get down on the floor. When I did, the incision on that recently operated knee opened just a little bit, but I didn't give it much thought. I put antibiotic ointment with a Band-Aid on it and continued to work. We put the floor down, completed the job, got paid and went on to buy more tools then go to a second job. We pulled into the pawn shop looking for tools and when we left, I put the truck into reverse. And just like, that I didn't have a reverse. I heard a voice just as clear as I'm talking, "You WILL be still." The Lord was telling me not to go out to work but I was bent on doing it. I went in the hole from that floor job because I would have to replace the transmission on my truck.

I kept ointment and a Band-Aid on that knee for a few days. Although it was warm weather, when I woke up that night I was freezing. I turned on the heater and put more blankets on the bed. Even my teeth were chattering. Tracy said, "Okay let's go to the ER and see what's going on." They ran all kinds of labs and tests and found a staph infection in my knee. Here I am in this messed up situation. I'm broke, the transmission on my truck is out, and now I have staph in my knee. Then I heard it again, "You WILL be still." I was admitted to the hospital on December 24, 2018, where I had more surgery on the same knee. I stayed in the hospital through my birthday, December 19, through Christmas and New Year's, 2019.

The doctors put me on infusion antibiotics. No one knew I was allergic to the antibiotic I was getting around the clock until, as I was getting back into bed from the chair, Tracy noticed my skin was coming off on my back and I was red all over. Tracy and the nurse were saying it was the fever and infection. Then I started breaking out in large blisters all over my body. My eyelids, cheeks, neck, stomach, legs, and back were a hot mess. Finally, it was determined that I was having a severe reaction to the antibiotic:

Redman's Syndrome. Immediately I was taken off it and different IV drip was started. For two months I was in the hospital. I thought to myself, okay, I wonder if Job felt this way with boils all over this body (Job 2:7—NIV: So Satan went out from the presence of the Lord and afflicted Job with painful sores from the soles of his feet to the crown of his head.

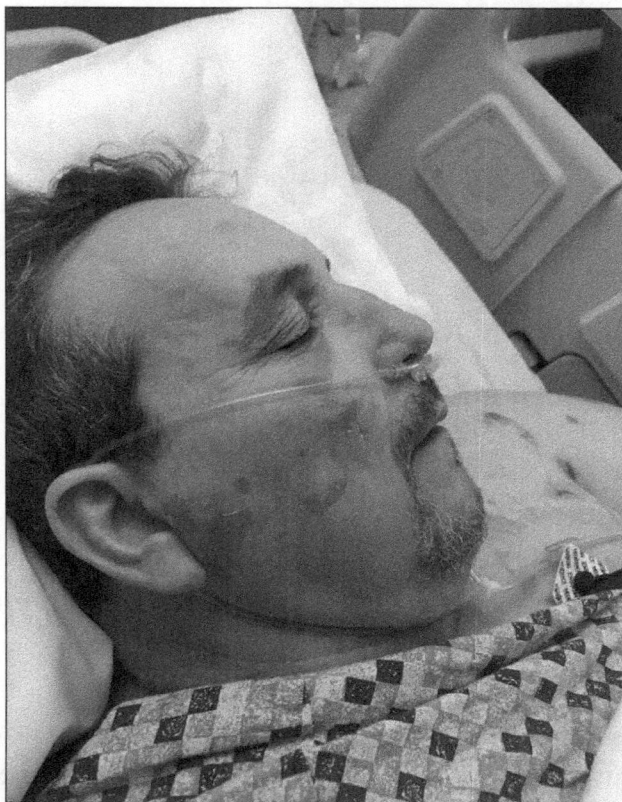

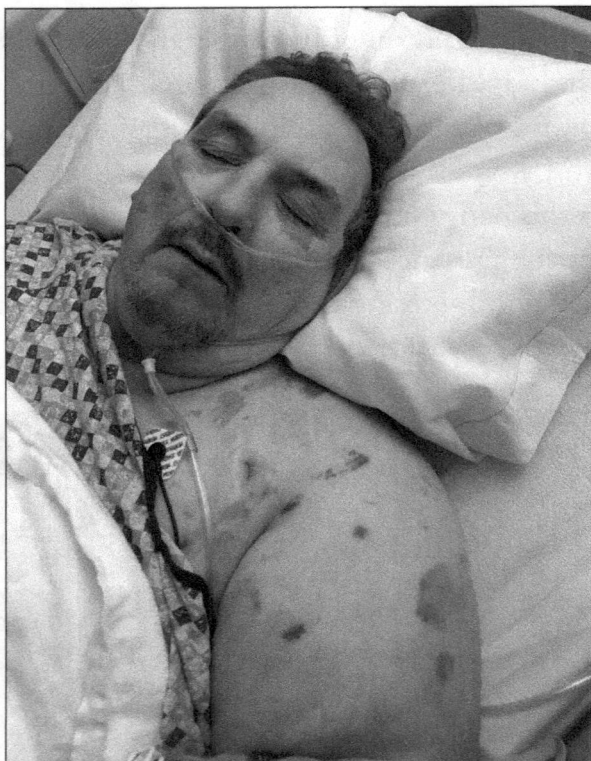

But I will not curse God. Shedding all that skin was like God has surely given me a new skin and is causing me to be still. After being released from the hospital I had to continue antibiotic infusion for six weeks. Everyday when Tracy came home from work, we would go to the hospital for an hour and a half for the infusion. It was a long, drawn out process for my recovery and, during that process, I learned that I have not outlived my past reputation in my little town. I needed to get those antibiotic infusions at the local hospital. Here I am at 60 years-old. I have been clean and sober for twelve years. The hospital would not take me because I had a reputation for being mean to the nurses.

Chapter Fifteen

A NOTHER HEALTH ISSUE:
"After the knee-infection fiasco, my heart started acting up. I was already on high powered heart medications, a defibrillator, and a pacemaker. My defibrillator started firing off one day. In the ER, it shocked me 27 times. I was exhausted by the time the doctor was finally able to get it to stop. Another doctor came in to check the bypass I had in 2000. The test results were as clear as if I just had them, the doctor said. He drew a graph of what he saw. At the bottom right of my heart was an extra graph that the doctor said he could not explain. Naturally I said, "I can explain it. That's my God!" Since the doctor increased the heart medication, I have done well in that area. Then the cardiologist that checks on the electrical part of my heart tells me, "Dennis we have to talk. Several years ago, I strongly suggested that you go to Pennsylvania to have a heart ablation and you refused." The doctor was serious on this and I asked him about the pros and cons of the procedure. He said I would be coming off almost all

the meds and I would have no more shocks from the defibrillator. That sounded wonderful!

I was thinking, 'Yes I could get this done then I can go back to work!' But he also heard the voice of the Lord say, "You will not work in that manner. I have a job for you to do."

A few weeks passed and my cardiologist called me in for an EKG. He explained the results: "A regular EKG goes up and down, Dennis, and—yours is mostly just a line; the pacemaker and high-powered meds are keeping you alive." Reality kicked in: we MUST go to Pennsylvania for an ablation. But I just had to ask THE question: Why all the way to Pennsylvania? Why not local, Atlanta or Augusta, where I had had two other ablations. The kind doctor said, "Your heart is complex and I need the <u>very best</u> specialist to touch you."

For the next month, Tracy and I worked on getting ready for the trip. The appointment was set for May 31, 2019. We knew we didn't have the funds to go and stay about two weeks, therefore, a Go Fund Me account was set up explaining the procedure and anticipated necessities as follows:

FEARLESS
–Brock Durden

"As many of you may know, Dennis has had problems with his heart and has been hospitalized several times over the past year. Due to recent findings, Dennis' cardiologist has decided to pass his case on to a cardiac-electro physiologist in Pennsylvania where he will have a cardiac ablation. Due to this urgent procedure, Dennis' wife, Tracy, must take time off from work for several weeks to accompany Dennis. Their son, Juston, will go with them. At the recommendation of his doctor, Dennis' recovery period will take a few days longer extending the family's stay in Pennsylvania. I am asking for donations on behalf of Dennis, Tracy and Juston to help provide gasoline, hotel, and food expenses for their trip to Pennsylvania.

I have known Dennis for quite some time. I have seen Dennis at his worst and at his best. Dennis has become a remarkably mighty man of God who has withstood, with God's mighty hand, the inevitable. Facing death numerous times, God has intervened on Dennis' behalf because he has a purpose and destiny to fulfill as a mighty man of God. To hear Dennis' testimony, only then will you be able to see and visualize what the mighty hand of God has done in his life and understand the greatness, power and purpose that God has bestowed upon Dennis. Spiritually, Dennis and Tracy know there is more to this journey than

God's using doctors to repair Dennis' heart. They have accepted this journey as a mandated mission from the Father, the Great I AM. Dennis, Tracy and Juston have extended their appreciation for all your prayers during their journey. The title of this fundraiser fits Dennis, because with God being the head of Dennis' life, Dennis is FEARLESS.

Deuteronomy 31:8—It is the Lord who goes before you; He will be with you. He will not fail you or abandon you. Do not fear or be dismayed."

God is good and has a plan; what another life-expedition this trip would be. On May 28, 2019, Tracy and I, with our son, Juston, left our hometown for Philadelphia, Pennsylvania, fully funded and then some as God met our needs just as He promised in Philippians 4:19. The ablation was scheduled for May 31.

Tracy continues our story:

In North Carolina, we stayed overnight. Juston had done a beautiful job driving us, paying attention to every detail, alert to every movement on the road. This was an exciting trip for us. We saw things we had never seen before and stopped to enjoy a few interesting sights while we rested.

Dennis was admitted to the University of Pennsylvania hospital on May 31 for his ablation.

Juston and I bided our time in the waiting room. We watched other people as they also waited with or for word about their loved ones. There was one lady whose husband was having the same procedure as Dennis. I could see anxiety on her face. After a while I went to her and introduced myself. Apparently needing someone to talk to, the lady began to say what all was going on with her husband. As I listened to her, I also listened for the Father's voice for the words of peace and comfort to say to the lady that would help to calm her storm of fear and anxiety as well as the uncertainty of not knowing whether her husband was going to be okay. I didn't want to say the wrong thing.

The lady talked about the doctors' visits, the hospital stays, and all the stress of worrying. I asked if I could pray with her. The look on her face was of relief that someone finally understood what she was going through. I asked if I could hold her hand while I prayed. "Yes, of course!" she said. It was amazing to see the blanket of peace come over her and the distress abate. The tears stopped flowing and a smile touched her lips. As we hugged, she thanked me and we went our separate ways. We would pass each other in the hall, see each other in the cafeteria, and spend a few moments visiting and sharing about the progress of our husbands over those few days.

After Dennis' 8 ½ hour procedure, the doctor came out with a face as red as fire. He was exhausted but delivered good news. He said he had done the best that he thought he could. He went on to explain the procedure. The heart is a muscle so imagine a piece of steak that he had to sear off the dead muscle around and under the heart. He had to be very slow and easy all the way around and under. He said, "So, we will see tomorrow when they interrogate his heart." That was to see if the defibrillator would fire and if the pacemaker would appropriately pace. When the heart was tested, the heart muscle performed perfectly—the ablation was a success!

Looking at the before and after EKGs, Dennis and I marvel at what God has done to bring healing. All the car wrecks, gunshots, fights, drug and alcohol abuse from an early age—it is amazing to think of where we are in relation to where we have been!

Nurse Barbara shared with Tracy that there are so many patients per nurse. The nurses would argue about who would get me. They said I was entertaining, full of life, and without complaint which was refreshing when the other patients were so sick and needy. Whoever came to check on me would come often just to hear me talk with my southern drawl. I was always nice and polite and would tell my old crazy, comical red-neck stories, just to be talking. I ate up the attention.

One of the nurses, Laynie, would look at me, smile and then say, "I wish I had a remote control so I could rewind you!" (What she was saying is that she couldn't understand my southern accent and if she could listen several times she probably could get it!)

Tracy said, "Everyone from the doctors, nurses or any one that had anything to do with Dennis was exceptional in their care and attention. Today, December 2019, Dennis' health is greater than anything it has been in a long while. He can do things he enjoys doing. He regularly goes to church when, a year ago, he could hardly get out of the house. He has a shop behind the house and that's his happy place. He goes out there and fiddles with any and everything that needs mechanical attention: lawnmower, chainsaw, weed eater. He also enjoys carpentry and cooking. Just to see him up and out of the house swells my heart. We give all the glory to our Savior, Jesus Christ."

Chapter Sixteen

K AY TUCKER BECAME OUR FRIEND WHEN WE
found out we were neighbors at the same apartment
complex in April 2010. She recalls:

> "I knew Tracy because I went to church with her.
> Because people talk and it's a very small town, I
> had heard of Dennis' reputation. I heard that back
> in his younger days, he was really rowdy and didn't
> walk away from a fight."

Kay shares her feeling that I was being unfaithful to Tracy:

> "I had seen a white car drive up not quite to where
> the apartment buildings stood. I saw Dennis get
> out of the car and walk up to a door on that end. I
> told Tracy what I had seen and she said she knew
> it. I wouldn't be near him when it looked like there
> was nobody around but the two of us. I knew he
> was involved with drugs. He had knocked on my
> door one day and had small kitchen appliance
> in his hand. He told me how nice it was and he
> asked me if I wanted to buy it. I knew it was
> Tracy's. He said, "I'll sell it to you for $10." I told
> him I had no use for it. Then he asked me to

hold it and lend him $10. Despite his persistence, I wasn't going to buy it. When I told him I had no money, he left. I called Tracy about it and she said she had been missing some things. She knew Dennis had pawned them to get drug money."

The morning that Dennis died I was just up and around piddling with nothing on my schedule. I heard someone running outside, then there was frantic beating on my door and I heard Tracy screaming hysterically. She was crying and she said, "It's Dennis, it's Dennis." I thought he had jumped on her and hurt her. She pleaded with me to hurry so I just closed my door and ran behind her to her house.

Dennis was sitting slumped over in a rocking chair. His eyes were cracked opened just a little and he wasn't breathing. His skin was an ugly white almost a greenish undertone and pasty looking. In my mind I thought, "I guess he's calmed down." That is when Tracy said, "He's dead! He's not breathing, he's dead!" Tracy was so in shock that when I asked if she had called an ambulance, she said she didn't have a phone book. I told her to just call 9-1-1. When I asked what happened, she said she didn't know. She had been in the kitchen and she just heard a strange noise she had never heard before, like a gurgle, in the living room where Dennis was sitting in his recliner. She went to check on Dennis. His head was slumped to the side and he had turned a gray color.

While Tracy was talking with EMS, I started praying for him and I said, "Dennis, I know your spirit can hear me. I started laying hands on him. I said you will surely live and not die and I started rebuking the spirit of death and calling on the Lord to bring life back into him. I kept telling Dennis to call out to Jesus.

Tracy got off the phone with 9-1-1. I was directly in front of Dennis and she was behind him. I had my hand on his chest and he started moving his head a little. When he opened his eyes, he had the wildest look that really scared me. I said, "Dennis ask the Lord to forgive you of your sins," and he said, "Forgive me, Jesus, please forgive me, Jesus."

When he died his bodily functions released and it wasn't but a very short time before the ambulance came. The EMT came in, attended Dennis and asked him if he could stand up. Dennis stood and the EMT instructed him to lie down on the stretcher, but Dennis was concerned that his clothes were messed up. The EMT said it was all right and they would fix it.

As I walked back home, the whole scenario played in my mind. I thought that if we had not been praying for him, he would not have come back to life. This was our faith at work. We believed and trusted in God to restore life. Tracy and I have continued to be friends. We continue to attend church services together. Looking back at that time when Dennis was in the world and to see him today as he participates in church activities and serving God makes my heart smile.

Chapter Seventeen

⟺

CLOSING REMARKS:

Since I have been born from above, I love everyone just as God commands. I found that people are not my enemy. Satan's tools can include people coming against us. People are never the enemy but allow themselves to be used as such. We must come against the darkness that drives them. The Bible says in Ephesians that our struggle is not with flesh and blood but with the powers of darkness. I am a threat to the devil and I expect his big guns in my face every day. However, the Bible also says, "Greater is He that is within me than he that is in the world."

Now I am removed from things that I wasn't before. I enjoy watching preaching and teaching on television. I cannot seem to watch much of the news. I watch just enough to know what is going on in the world. I have a hunger to learn things about God. Even my wife says I am more loveable today. I regret not knowing the love of God like I do now so that my two sons could have benefitted.

Pray and obey and God will take care of your every need. This takes exercising your faith which is like a muscle, the more it is used the stronger it gets. Don't get comfortable or complacent. God is a God that shall not lie, He is merciful, faithful, and wonderful. Stand on His word. He gives us instructions on how to live. He wants to bless us. Our minds cannot comprehend what He has in store for us.

It takes a relationship. We must get to know Him. He is everywhere we are. I must crucify my flesh daily. This flesh is hard, it stinks, and it's ugly. Deny it daily, pick up the cross and follow Him.

Conclusion

———•———

ACCORDING TO MERRIAM-WEBSTER, THE definition of the word *conclusion* is *the last part of something; the result; or outcome.* My testimony cannot be concluded because the story is not finished. God has a mighty plan, a destiny, laid out for me to fulfil so the Kingdom of God is increased. Psalms 37:23-24 says *The steps of a good man are ordered of the Lord; and He delights in his way. Though he fall, he shall not be utterly cast down, for the Lord upholds him with His hand.* Psalms 23:4 says *Yea, though I walk through the valley of the shadow of death, I will fear no evil; for You are with me; Your rod and staff comfort me.*

I pray my story is one that will reach a hurting and dying generation as well as generations to come. My testimony will minister to the hurting, the dying, the ones who feel worthless, that God is right there with them and has always been with them, with arms wide open ready to love them and use them, despite the mess and chaos that weighs them down.

From the time I was a toddler until my late 40s, my choices, reactions, and dysfunctional life condemned me until I became acquainted with Romans 8:1, "*There is now no condemnation, no guilty verdict, no punishment for those who are in Christ Jesus who believe in Him as personal Lord and Savior."*

Just like every Christian, I still deal with overcoming sin, but through the work of the Holy Spirit, we can be free from the control of sin. The mind of the flesh pursues sin; but the mind of the Spirit is life and peace, the spiritual well-being that comes from walking with God, both now and forever.

All spirits of resentment, hurt, rejection, control and many more have been a part of my life. No matter what path I walked down, God has always been ahead of me. All the boulders and mountains, God had already gone ahead and maneuvered over and around them. I didn't always realize it, but all during my misfit lifestyle, God was with me.

The many stories of my life could be parables. They are embarrassing and humiliating true events with something to learn from each. This is a healing work for me. It has been my Damascus Road—before Jesus opened my eyes. I want you to see that God loves me and has always been with me. God loves you and is with you, too, even if you do not yet recognize Him or His love. I feel like I've been to Hell and back because of the pain of my family break-up and the treatment I got from my step-family as well as other people. It is my heart's desire for you to know that you don't have to live in shame and you can be set free.

Encouraging words from my wife:

"God knows right where we all are. It's not by chance you are where you are. God has you right where He wants you. Know and believe this— wherever you are, there is NO condemnation even in your mess. Whatever your struggles, throw up your hands and say aloud, "Lord, help me. You made me. You are an all-knowing God. Help me have a changed mind set. Take out of my mouth the taste that is not pleasing to you, in Jesus Name." Praise Him in the middle of your storm. Lock your wings as an eagle soars above the storm to the top of the mountain and be restored in Jesus name. Satan is a liar!!"

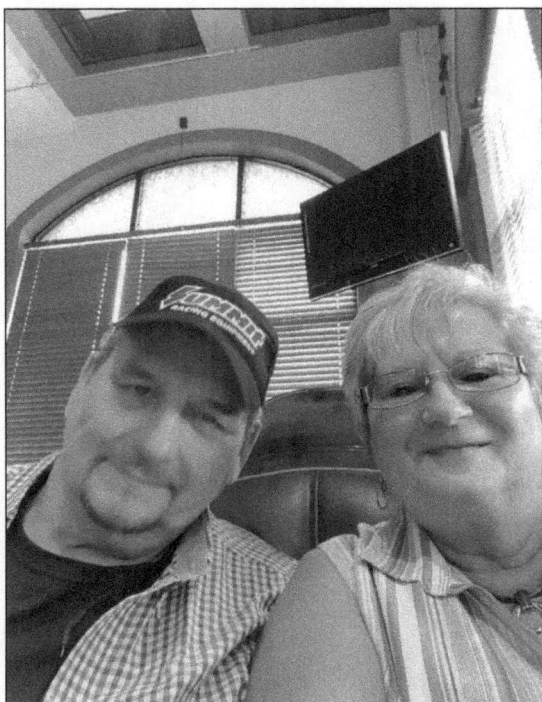

References Cited

cdc.gov/tb/worldtbday/history.htm. Retrieved 9/11/2020

Eldridge, John. *Wild at Heart.* (Nashville: Thomas Nelson, Inc., 2001), pp. 65-70.

En.wikipedia.org/siki/Hunter_Army_Airfield. Retrieved 01/17/2020.

Epp, Theodore. *Practical Studies in Revelation, Volume 1.* (Lincoln, Nebraska: Back to the Bible Broadcast, 1969)

Grace, Amanda. Amanda Grace Talks...Prophetic Teaching: Staying the Course During the Enemy's Attempts, A New Chapter. YouTube, 2019.

National Vital Statistics System. (1980). Marriages: Trends and Characteristics, United States. (Series 21, Number 21, page 11)

Wright, Henry W. (1999). *A More Excellent Way.* Pennsylvania: Whitaker House.

Acknowledgements

S PECIAL THANKS TO MY WIFE, TRACY, WHO stayed on top of contributing information as well as the status of this book. She kept pushing even in the hard times: if the enemy could cause division between us, Tracy was on top of it making peace in the house.

There are several others:

-My niece, Lila Ann Durden, who always spoke positive words into my life. She once told me people were waiting for me to get this book out for their breakthrough.

-My niece, Michelle Coursey, her daughter, Shanna, and friend, Stefanie Finch for designing a GoFundMe page for the contributions to help with the cost of publishing. Stefanie designed the title and front cover for me. She was always encouraging and willing to do anything to help me.

-Jason Caron, publishing consultant at Xulon Press, has been an encouragement daily or weekly by text or phone.

-My friends, family, and church family who were always giving God the glory investing in the Kingdom and praying for this venture.

-Carol Montgomery who God placed before me about three years ago at a home Bible study group. After hearing a few facts of my story, she said I needed to write a book. What she didn't know was God had already told me to do it. She enjoys writing and offered to interview friends, family, and acquaintances. I cried remembering the hurts and dark places I had to talk about and she cried as my story impacted her and areas of her life. Philippians 1:6 says, "I am convinced and sure that He who began a good work in me will continue until the day of Jesus Christ, developing and perfecting and bringing it to full completion in me." Many thanks to Carol for the time she spent with us helping to get my story into the book you just read.

-Kay Tucker, whom Tracy and I met 11 years ago, is an accountability partner. Kay has seen me at my lowest and where I stand today. She is a steadfast friend that prays for my family as we pray for hers.

-Richard Johnson, my brother, has seen just about all the good, bad and ugly, for both of us, as we share a lot of the same story. He remembered happenings that I didn't which contributed tremendously to this book.

-Sheriff Homer Bell (retired) so graciously although hesitantly gave an interview agreeing with all that was written law enforcement-wise. While he didn't remember some things, he did say "That sounds about right". When asked why he went to such great lengths to help people like

Dennis, he lauded his own father's example as "That's the way I was taught."

-Brother Warren (deceased now) and Sister Bonnie Warren always loved me as one of their own sons and helped me pick up the broken pieces many times. "Mom Preacher" to me, Sister Bonnie told me I had to carry on Brother Warren's mantle of encouraging the meanest and helping others to pick up the pieces.

-David Aldrich, step-cousin, but every bit as committed as my own blood. He has seen the roads I have travelled, both good and bad, and even participated in a few trips. His encouragement has been priceless.

-Ricky Brantley who, at one time, didn't want anything to do with me. He said I was too mean to die. Over the years we became the best of friend. He is my mentor today and we talk daily. He encourages me, backs me up, and tells me what I need to hear whether or not I want to hear it.

Summary

Tossed to and fro in a sea of dysfunctional living throughout the years, it has taken almost a lifetime for me to find direction. As a toddler I began learning to deal with the everyday challenges of confusion and abuse. With no one to lead me, I naively followed the obvious broad paths to destruction. Regardless of the challenge in the battles and trials I faced, they shaped my purpose and direction in life. The hardships were not wasted; the pains had purpose.

I believed I had a reputation of toughness to uphold which included alcohol and drug abuse. I walked through fire regardless of the fuel. Because of the decisions of my immature, ignorant, and willful self, I should have been maimed for life or even killed. I have been raised from the dead three times. This gradually caused me to realize there was a Power much greater than me with a purpose I would eventually realize.

If it had not been for the effectual, fervent prayers of my wife and the body of Christ who relentlessly prayed for me, I might still be a source of grave concern today. Each of my family members, blood and step-, eventually came to the saving knowledge of Jesus Christ. If God never does another thing for me, I know He has already used my life to bring others to Him.

CPSIA information can be obtained
at www.ICGtesting.com
Printed in the USA
LVHW041643020621
689155LV00005B/239

9 781662 817762